D1707301

The New Americans
Recent Immigration and American Society

Edited by
Steven J. Gold and Rubén G. Rumbaut

A Series from LFB Scholarly

Women, Migration, and Domestic Work on the Texas-Mexico Border

Christina Mendoza

LFB Scholarly Publishing LLC
El Paso 2011

Copyright © 2011 by LFB Scholarly Publishing LLC

Library of Congress Cataloging-in-Publication Data

Mendoza, Christina, 1975-
  Women, migration, and domestic work on the Texas-Mexico border /
Christina Mendoza.
      p. cm. -- (The new Americans: recent immigration and American
society)
  Includes bibliographical references and index.
  ISBN 978-1-59332-457-5 (hbk. : alk. paper)
  1. Women foreign workers--Mexican-American Border Region. 2.
Women household employees--Mexican-American Border Region. 3.
Foreign workers, Mexican--United States. 4. Mexican-American
Border Region--Emmigration and immigration--Social aspects. 5.
Mexican-American Border Region--Emmigration and immigration--
Economic aspects. I. Title.
  HD8081.M6M36 2011
  331.4'86409721--dc22
                                        2011002368

ISBN 978-1-59332-457-5

Printed on acid-free 250-year-life paper.

Manufactured in the United States of America.

To Lalith, Antonio, and Sofia
with all my love

Table of Contents

vii

Acknowledgements

This study could not have been completed without the encouragement and support of many people. I must first thank all of the women in Laredo and Nuevo Laredo who had the courage to open up their homes and their hearts to me to participate in this study. I am eternally grateful to each of you and I hope I do justice to the stories and life experiences you shared with me.

I am thankful for the financial support of many University of Michigan funders, namely: Rackham Merit Fellowship, the Institute for Research and Gender Community of Scholars Program, the International Institute Global Transformation Seminar, and the Department of Sociology. In addition, I grateful for the generous support of the Chicana/Latina Research Center at University of California, Davis who provided both funds for writing and research.

I am also extremely grateful to my teachers and mentors whose knowledge and guidance made the completion of this study possible. Jayati Lal, Sonya O. Rose, Maria Cotera, Michael Kennedy, Maria Montoya, Ines Hernadez Avila, and Jeffrey Halley.

I am also gracious to Jassenth Torres and Lucia Hernandez, who assisted in the fieldwork and data collection, and to Maria Pilar Flynn, Sara A. Mendoza, and Swapnaa Jayaraman, who assisted in the interview transcriptions. Finally, I am thankful for the unending support of my colleagues, family, and friends.

CHAPTER 1

Women's Migration and Domestic Service

Introduction

Late on the night of September 16, 2006, Congress approved the Secure Fence Act, authorizing the construction and partial funding of a 700 mile long fence along the United States-Mexico border, sending a clear message on the United States' stance on illegal immigration from Mexico and the effort to secure the nation's borders. This barrier, which would cost an estimated 2 to 7 billion dollars to construct, would include 370 miles of a triple-layer 15 foot fence, 330 miles of virtual fence, and a network of cameras, high-tech sensors, radars, and other sophisticated technology. The approval of this border wall reflects the strong anti-immigration sentiments across the country that are pressuring lawmakers to take action against the continued flow of undocumented immigration from Mexico.[1]

However, across the Texas-Mexico border, communities are outraged over the passage of this act, calling this fence a "slap in the face" to the Mexican community, which they rely upon for business and trade, and with whom they have co-existed side-by-side for centuries. In reaction to the passage of this legislation, border cities have enacted resolutions opposing this wall and city mayors have banded together to protest the construction of this physical barrier, which they say will sour their relationship with Mexico and threaten shared wildlife habitats. The Mexican community has dubbed this planned fence a "wall of shame."

U.S. border cities are intimately familiar with the economic stress that unauthorized immigrants place on their communities. These communities continually struggle with overburdened hospitals, crowded schools, and other strains on public assistance that are often attributed to the growing increase of unauthorized persons from Mexico. In spite of these burdens immigrants pose to these communities, why do border cities oppose legislation that would seemingly protect their interests? Will such physical

---

[1] In this study, I use undocumented and unauthorized interchangeably. I define these terms using the definition of the Pew Hispanic Research Center (Passel 2006) which states, "Unauthorized migrant to mean a person who resides in the United States but who is not a U.S. citizen, has not been admitted for permanent residence, and is not in a set of specific authorized temporary statuses permitting longer-term residence and work."

barriers curb the tide of illegal immigration as the government claims it will? And, is the border really such a different place from the rest of the United States?

In this study, I attempt to address these questions by examining the migration of a subset of the population of Mexican migrants and border community members who are deeply involved in these processes of migration.[2] While most studies on Mexican immigration examine cities in the interior of the United States, this study stays at the border, examining migration and the social conditions of undocumented Mexican domestic workers on both sides of this political and geographic divide, which are separated only by the Rio Grande River. This study examines the cross-border migration by Mexican women, who reside in Mexico and commute to American border cities to work in domestic service. This approach to migration provides insight into the motivations and behaviors of workers, who choose to migrate locally, and to employers, who fuel this cross-border movement of Mexican laborers. Through the analysis of these groups, I am approaching the questions posed above from a variety of angles, with a main focus on

---

[2] Throughout this study I repeatedly use the words *migration* and *immigration*. I use the word migration to refer to the movement of individuals or groups across national boundaries, and immigrant typically means those who enter into and settle in a nation other than their native country. But these terms are complicated by the frequent movement of persons back and forth, to and from their native countries across the world; taking this into consideration, Roger Rouse (1995) transforms this word to "(im)migration" as a means to account for the fluctuating status of individuals in relation to their movement.

understanding Mexican women's migration at the borderlands of these two nations.

I first began thinking about migrant labor at the border after reading Evelyn Nakano Glenn's (1992) seminal article on the intersection of race and gender in women's waged reproductive labor, "From Servitude to Service Work: Historical Continuities in the Racial Division of Paid Reproductive Labor." After reading this article, I began to think about the large population of Mexican domestic workers in my own hometown of Laredo, Texas. Growing up in this border city, I was very familiar with Mexican 'maids,' as they are referred to locally, who comprise an integral part of the fabric of daily life for border city residents. In this community, most members of the middle and upper-classes hire some form of undocumented paid domestic help; their labor is an unquestioned and normalized aspect of community life in the city. They are also a very visible aspect of life in Laredo, as they answer doors and take phone messages in their employer's homes, and are seen waiting for local buses across town. Yet, at the same time, as a form of migration, this phenomenon has been invisible in the sense that their labor and presence in local homes is taken for granted as nothing unusual. Spending most of my life within this "border culture" forced me to closely consider this migrant population of women anew. As I will describe in the next section, a significant number of Mexican women in Laredo, as in other border cities, commute from their homes in Mexico on a daily basis to work in domestic service on the American side of the border. As I began thinking about this process and experience of migration, I found that the interdisciplinary literature on migration did not examine this form of temporary and recursive movement across borders as it has relied on the framework of settlement. Most of the literature, especially that involving Mexican immigration, understands the migratory process as either a long-term or cyclical experience, such as the history of agricultural workers which is based on the male migrant experience. Additionally, the experiences of Mexican women laborers are most often understood as a migration for maintaining family unity and not for their own labors. What are the material and social conditions that influence some women to immigrate into and later settle in the U.S., and others to become long-term commuters? How are the meanings of social spaces—such as that of 'home,' the 'workspace,' and the spaces in-between—transformed by this frequent movement of workers? And how does this cross-border movement shape the meaning and structure of co-ethnic employee/employer relationships?

In the following sections, I delve deeper into the literature that informs these topics of domestic labor and migration of women, and the questions that are driving these inquiries, particularly as they relate to the Mexican migratory experience.

This study explores the temporary migration of Mexican women who reside in Mexican border cities and travel daily to American border cities to labor in domestic service. Based on in-depth interviews and participant observation with domestic workers, employers, and community members in the paired border cities of Laredo, Texas and Nuevo Laredo, Mexico, I study this frequent movement across international borders to analyze how this movement creates and reinforces inequalities of class, gender, and nationality in these borderlands.

This study explores three distinct but interrelated themes regarding Mexican women's migration. First, I examine the pre-emigration context that drives Mexican women to temporarily migrate as undocumented domestic laborers to border cities in the United States. I do so by analyzing the social and economic conditions in Mexico that have motivated working-class women to seek employment outside their country. Second, I analyze the recurrent movement of women crossing international borders, whose legal entry into U.S. border cities is complicated by their undocumented employment in domestic service. This pseudo-legal migration creates a space wherein different areas represent "safe" and "risky" zones for the cross-border worker. Finally, I examine the (re)production of difference by domestic workers and employers. I explore how borders and boundaries in the lives of cross-border workers span the political divide that they cross daily and permeate the dynamics between workers and employers. I deploy the concept of symbolic boundaries to analyze the production of difference and how difference is negotiated in the relations between Mexican domestic workers and Mexican American employers.

This study makes a contribution to the discipline of sociology by examining the temporary migration of workers, which has been largely absent in the scholarship of migration. The movement of these women contributes to an understanding of the social inequalities embedded their migration and their labor as workers. It also brings attention to the inequalities of social class, gender, and nationality among co-ethnic women, who are typically essentialized in the literature and seen as a homogeneous group. Mexican women migrants are understudied in traditional sociological research. Women who emigrate from Mexico to the United States have been by and large depicted primarily as passive actors in migratory decisions, where the male head of household chooses and evaluates the best option for the family (Cerrutti & Massey 2001; Mines & Massey 1985). By focusing on temporary migration, this study contributes to a perspective on Mexican women migrants that sees them as active agents in their decisions to cross the border (Hirsh 1999; Hondagneu-Sotelo 1994), and to pursue higher-waged employment outside their home country. My study also draws on and contributes to the interdisciplinary fields of women's studies and the borderlands literature. Women's studies scholarship on the border has been predominantly humanistic and lacks an empirical basis in the social sciences, while the latter has been predominantly undertaken by geographers who also do not draw on qualitative scholarship on communities and specific groups of migrants. While I draw on this literature in my conceptualization of the 'border zones,' I hope to address this lacuna in these literatures as well.

Women's Migration and Settlement

The United Nations defines a migrant worker as "a person who is engaged or has been engaged in a remunerated activity in a State of which he or she is not a national" (United Nations 1990). This definition is broad and encompasses a variety of foreign workers in the United States. In studies on immigrant women workers, settlement is inextricably linked to migration and is an implicit framework for understanding women's migratory experiences in the United States. Evelyn Nakano Glenn (1986) refers to Japanese women's entry into the U.S. as the "settlement period" in which marked the start of the establishment of families and community for three future generations of immigrant women. In her study on the gender dynamics and migration of Mexican men and women, Hondagneu-Sotelo (1994) asserts that immigrant women are central to Mexican migrant settlement in the United States and analyzes how gender operates within this settlement framework.

The framework of settlement is also imbedded in recent studies on transnationalism. In the last decade, social scientists have sought to understand the migrant experience by examining the connections between migrant host societies and sending. In their original conceptualization of the term transnationalism, Linda Basch, Nina Glick Schiller, and Cristina Szanton Blanc (1994) defined this phenomena as "processes by which immigrants forge and sustain multi-stranded social relations that link together their societies of origin and settlement" (7). Since the introduction of this term, the study of transnationalism has moved in many different directions and scholars have attempted to redefine and place limitations on this term (Levitt & Jaworsky 2007). Nonetheless, the study of transnationalism challenges the geographic boundaries of space and the social identities of those individuals whose daily activities and subjectivities are embedded in two different nations (Basch et. al 1994; Faist 2000; Glick Schiller et. al 1992). This body of literature is especially important to my study because it considers the social spaces in which migrants actively participate as fluid and constantly negotiated as result of their simultaneous involvement in both communities (Levitt & Glick Schiller 2004, Smith 2005). Yet studies using the term transnationalism continue to frame cross-border activities as specific to long-term immigrants, and typically do not explore the frequent movement of workers as a form of this transnational activity.

A few scholars have moved beyond the settlement model. Specifically, Aihwa Ong (1999) challenged the assumption of settlement in migrant experiences in her study Flexible Citizenship, where she analyzes the frequent movement of globe-trotting Hong Kong business men. In her study, these hyper-mobile managers and technocrats are "seeking both to circumvent and benefit from different state regimes by selecting different sites for investment, work, and family relocations" (112). The border crossings Ong describes are limited to a select class of privileged members of the business class whose movement across borders is legal and free of restrictions. Sarah Mahler (2003) also analyzes the frequent movement of workers in her analysis of "transnational couriers," who travel monthly from El Salvador to the United States and back to transport remittances, packages, and other goods. She found that a large segment of these couriers were middle-aged women who were able to successfully move across these spaces by establishing sustained social networks in both countries. This study expands on the migration literature by analyzing cross-border domestic workers who "migrate" across international divides without the intension of settlement.

Women, Migration, and the Global Economy

In order to understand the movement of cross-border domestic workers in this study, it is important to review the larger scholarship on women's migration to better understand the multiple factors that motivate this form of migration. Before the 1980s, women were generally absent from the literature on migration. Many scholars during this time were influenced by neo-classical theories, which examined migration using supply and demand of international labor and changes in wages upon migration to understand migratory experiences (Pessar 1999). Under these "push and pull" models, women's migration was unimportant and invisible, especially for those women who worked in the private sector and whose wages were not counted (Momsem 1999). Women migrants were also considered passive, in that males were the deciding actors in the migration of family members and that when women did migrate it was to follow men (Pedraza 1991). During this period, women's participation in economic, political, and social life was also ignored (Pessar 1999). In these studies, migration was considered a phenomenon experienced by men, and, if women were included, they were assumed to share the same experiences as men. As a result of the absence of women in this body of research, the general aim of studies that followed was to "add" women to this scholarship, specifically by collecting data on women and comparing these results to that of male migrants (Hondagneu-Sotelo 2003).

The scholarship on women's migration took an important turn in the 1980s from the "add and stir" approach to shifting gender dynamics (Hondagneu-Sotelo 2003). Among the scholars who made this transition in the literature was Saskia Sassen (1998b), who linked the migratory movement of young women in areas with industrial manufacturing to the restructuring of the global economy. She found that when export-manufacturing expanded to developing countries, large proportions of women worked in these factories overseas. This employment mobilized women to migrate from rural to urban areas in their countries, and later to the United States.

This macro approach to women's migration and gender transformed the study of migration by incorporating the effect of globalization in the analysis of women's national and transnational movements. The case of Mexico is particularly important since it maintains the largest and longest sustaining migrant flow into the United States (Cerrutti & Massey 2001). Sassen (1998a) takes a close look at the U.S. immigration "problem" and suggests that the causes for migration, especially for women, are more complicated than the mainstream argument that explains the current migratory trends. She argues that a number of different factors are involved in women from less-developed countries seeking to emigrate to the U.S. First, the direct recruitment of young women in rural areas by industries in urban areas has led to a mass migration from rural to urban centers. The displacement of traditional unpaid work patterns performed by women has directly impacted the local economies. Rural women, a population who previously would not have entered the paid labor force, are no longer providing the necessary unpaid domestic labor needed for the production of goods and family services. With the exodus of this labor force into the public arena of work, the economies of these rural areas are shrinking, making it more difficult for these women to return once they are no longer employable in export-oriented industries (Sassen 1998b). With the disappearance of a traditional work structure, a pool of potential migrants is created. In the case of Mexico, the enactment of the Border Industrialization Project in 1965 initiated the movement of women workers who were previously located in the home to seek work at factories. Instead of hiring men who were displaced by the Bracero

Program (which I discuss at length in Chapter 3), these factories preferred the supposedly docile labor of young women (Fernandez-Kelly 1983; Kopinak 1995).[3] The enactment of the North American Free Trade Agreement (NAFTA) in 1993 expanded women's participation in export manufacturing industries (Kopinak 1995; Prieto 1997; Salzinger 2003). The policies have transformed the economies in Mexico, bringing women closer to the U.S.-Mexico border and making emigration a logical alternative to industrial work (Tiano 1994). Chapter 3 of this study analyzes in detail the multiple factors that influence the migration of Mexican women.

The literature on women's migration subsequently moved from the macro-perspective to a meso-level stage that included family-level analysis on the migratory patterns and inequalities of gender between men and women in the process of migration (Grasmuck & Pessar 1991; Kibria 1993; Hondagneu-Sotelo 1994). Although these studies contributed to a gendered understanding of migration at the household level, this level of analysis has been criticized for providing an incomplete perspective on the migration experience by not considering other institutions outside of the family that are also gendered—i.e. employment in a global labor market, immigration patterns, and citizenship (Hondagneu-Sotelo 2003). The recent wave of feminist migration studies understands

---

[3] Between 1983 and 1989, due to pressure from the International Monetary Fund (IMF), the Mexican government began supporting capital intensive maquiladoras, specifically those factories that specialized in machinery, electric and electronic supplies, and automotive equipment. At this time the proportion of women in the maquiladora labor force decreased (Fernandez-Kelly 1983).

gender as a constitutive element in the migration of women and men and incorporates gender at the individual, institutional, and economic levels (Parreñas 2001; Lan 2006). I apply this approach to women's migration in this study of the cross-border movement of domestic workers at the U.S.-Mexico border.

Migration and Domestic Work

Domestic work and migration are intimately connected. In order to understand the connections between migration and domestic work in my study on cross-border workers, the recent literature on domestic service serves as an important framework for understanding the influences of gender, class, race, and nationality on the relationships between employers and domestic workers, the structure of this labor, and entry of immigrant women into this occupation. Feminist scholars have thoroughly explored the importance of applying an intersectional perspective to examine the experiences of women of color in the United States (Collins 1999; Baca Zinn & Thornton Dill 1996; Mohanty 1991; Espiritu 1992). They contend that race and gender are socially constructed categories, which are fluid with multi-layered meanings, and they consider them to be so interwoven that race and ethnicity are understood as always inflected by gender (Collins 1999; Glenn 1999). Theories on intersections emphasize the power dynamics that are embedded in these social categories and the interconnection between privilege and disadvantage that race and gender reveal (Baca Zinn & Thornton Dill 1996; Glenn 1999; Higginbotham 1997). In the scholarship on women of color, such as on Latina domestic workers, who are typically from the working poor, women are understood as experiencing multiple disadvantages so that, along with race and gender, social class also functions as an intersecting axis of stratification (Segura 1989; Beal 1970).

The literature on paid domestic labor has adopted this approach to understand the experiences of domestic workers in the United States. Race, class, and gender are important in an examination of the relationships between employers and domestic workers, where employers are typically white and where domestic workers are Black (Rollins 1989; Dill 1988; Sutherland 1981; Palmer 1989), Asian (Glenn 1986), or Latina (Romero 1992; Hondagneu-Sotelo 2001). Several studies have also focused on these interconnections, especially since historically marginalized women have been disproportionately located in this occupation. For instance, after emancipation, Black women dominated paid domestic labor in the Southern United States and in some areas of the North. For generations, they continued working in domestic service because few other occupations were available to them. After the civil rights movement, Black women left the occupation in large numbers for clerical jobs and other careers (Sutherland 1981; Glenn 1986). European immigrants in the past have also worked as maids and housekeepers in the early years of their immigration, specifically a large number of Irish women who were employed in private homes in the North (Sutherland 1981; Diner 1983). Irish women were typically unmarried and migrated alone; entry into domestic work was thus not only practical, since they were provided with lodging and meals, but it also served as transitional work until they found a husband and/or more desirable employment (Steinberg 1981). Unlike North American minority women, European immigrants were typically able to escape the occupation after one generation (Sutherland 1981; Glenn 1992).

Along with the intersections of race, class, and gender, it is also necessary to incorporate an understanding of nationality to adequately grasp the experiences of women currently working in this occupation. Since women working in domestic service, especially at the border, typically do not have legal authorization to work in the United States, their nationality significantly impacts the ways in which inequalities of race, class and gender are embedded in this occupation. Domestic workers who are undocumented are vulnerable to exploitation and mistreatment by employers (Hondagneu-Sotelo 2001). In addition, the occupation of domestic work brings two distinct groups of women together in close and constant contact where perceptions of national distinctions can be a form of difference that affects these relationships. At the Texas-Mexico border, where this study takes place, nationality is especially important in understanding the relationships between employers and domestic workers, since in many border cities the majority of residents on the Texas side of the border identify as having Mexican ancestry. Sociologists Pablo Vila who examined the social categories and narrative identities of border inhabitants in El Paso, Texas, found that Mexican Americans in this border city "use nationality to detach themselves from Mexican nationals and to open a gap 'inside' the Mexican ethnic category" (Vila 2000, 83). With the growing number of women migrants from less developed countries entering the United States to work in the homes of middle and upper-class Americans, distinctions created by national differences must be included in the intersectionality framework of race, class, and gender which is typically employed in studies on domestic service.

Studies on the global migration of women across the world have transformed the literature on paid domestic labor in the United States. The changing global economy has created what has been termed the "new world domestic order" (Hondagneu-Sotelo 2001) in which the occupation of domestic work has expanded across industrialized countries such as the United States, Canada, and European nations along with oil rich countries in Asia and the Middle East. The growing demand for paid reproductive labor is being filled by women from Mexico, Central America, the Philippines, Sri Lanka and other impoverished countries around the world. In this international division of labor, the rapid industrialization of "core" nations, such as the United States, has created a need for foreign labor from nations in the "periphery" (Sassen-Koob 1983). The increased reliance on foreign labor in this occupation is central to understanding the experiences of contemporary domestic workers in nations across the world (Hondagneu-Sotelo 2001; Parreñas 2001; Lan 2006; Chang 2000; Constable 1997; Ehrenreich & Hochschild 2000; de la Luz Ibarra 2000; Momsem 1999).

Immigrant women from Mexico and other Latin American countries now comprise the majority of domestic workers in the United States. Domestic service is one of the few occupations available to undocumented women, making this group of women vulnerable to extremely low wages and exploitative working conditions. Often, employers justify paying their workers low wages by assuming that these women are better off working in the United States at these wages than they would be working in their home country (Hondagneu-Sotelo 2001). Because of the prevailing gender ideologies regarding domesticity, women have typically been the predominant workers in this sector. Inequalities of gender are inherent in this occupation. Women continue to be primarily responsible for the upkeep of the home and the care of children. Middle and upper-class American women seeking relief from the gendered expectations of the home rely on low-waged domestic labor. Mary Romero argues that paid domestic labor is a "contradiction in feminism" in that when women were encouraged to join the paid labor force outside the home, their reproductive labor became the responsibility of other women (1992: 98). Gender, race and ethnicity, class, and nationality work together in shaping the experiences and opportunities of women working in domestic service and the hierarchies between workers and employers. Because of the prevailing gender ideologies regarding domesticity, women have typically been the predominant workers in this sector.

Immigrant domestic workers also rely on the paid labor of other women to care for their families while they themselves are working in domestic service abroad (Hondagneu-Sotelo & Avila 1997; Parreñas 2001), creating what Rhacel Parreñas refers to as the "international transfer of caretaking" (2001: 62). Class is also germane in this occupation in that employers are clearly privileged when compared with their employees, who witness first-hand, and on a daily basis, the material differences in their social positions. The changing global economy has created what Maria de la Luz Ibarra (2000) has termed the "new domestic labor" in which the structure of social reproduction has been transformed. In the past, employing a paid household worker was a luxury afforded by solely the upper-class. However, due to the availability of low-waged immigrant labor, many middle class households can now afford housecleaning, full-time nannies, or elderly care workers. Women working in this occupation are also more diverse than in the past, with many educated women fleeing countries with few employment opportunities to work in domestic service. Parreñas refers to the large numbers of educated Filipina women employed in domestic service in Los Angeles and Rome as experiencing "contradictory class mobility," in which despite their higher levels of education, upon entering domestic service they experienced a significant decline in their social status in the receiving countries (2001: 3). The influx of women has also transformed the labor of domestic service in that the availability and affordability of this labor has created new categories of domestic labor (de la Luz Ibarra 2000).

The challenges immigrant women experience in maintaining a family in their home countries while they live and work across the border is a topic that has only recently been explored in studies on domestic work. Scholarship on gender and migration calls for an exploration of the transnational experiences of immigrant women (Pessar 2003). For example, in their study on Latina domestic workers, Pierrette Hondagneu-Sotelo and Ernestina Avila (1997) expand the study of motherhood and domestic service from the labor of mothering that is expected as part of the job of paid-nannies and housekeepers to include the "transnational mothering" that these women are engaged in with their own families living abroad. They found that women living away from their families advocate for more flexible definitions of motherhood and redefine the traditional standards of what it means to be a "good" mother. Transnational families are not a new phenomenon, but what is new is the rapid flow of information and money across these barriers (Parreñas 2001, Rouse 1992). Domestic workers, such as in the case of the Philippines, do not return home to their families for years, and instead continue living and working in the host country and supporting their family's daily expenses and all other financial needs. Visa regulations, the economy in their home country, their personal relationships with their spouses, and the geographic distance between the Philippines and their migratory country extend the stay of these women workers. Both parents and children in these families yearn to be united, but structural forces continue to keep them apart (Parreñas 2001). Recent feminist scholarship on paid domestic labor has thus brought attention to the formation of transnational families along with "new inequalities and new meanings in family life" that are a result of the restructuring of the global economy in which families in rich countries are privileged by the separation of families across the world (Hondagneu-Sotelo 2001: 27). In my study, the geographic distance between "home" and "work" for the cross-border workers is short, especially compared to Filipina women working abroad. But, the implications of crossing national boundaries are important to understanding the experiences of women in this occupation.

Crossing Borders

Today's nannies and maids in the United States migrate from the global south to the global north in search of employment. Women migrants are especially likely to seek out "global cities" to find work and eventually settle. These global cities are areas that "concentrate some of the global economies' key functions and resources," offering immigrant women an array of low-paying and unskilled jobs (Sassen 2003, p.255). Recent literature on domestic work has also paid particular attention to these large cities that have recently expanded along with the global economy. Places like Los Angeles (Parreñas 2001, Hondagneu-Sotelo 2001), Rome (Parreñas 2001), Hong Kong (Constable 1997), and Taiwan (Lan 2006) have been identified as areas with a significant number of migrant women in domestic service. These large global cities are not the only areas that serve as important regions in the expansion of the global economy; the U.S.-Mexico border also has an important and unique location site for migration and globalization. The U.S. is the busiest land border in the world with approximately 300 million people crossing this 2,000 mile divide every year (Andreas 2003: 6). Since the inception of NAFTA in 1993, trade between these two countries has increased exponentially from $81 billion to $332 billion in the year 2003 (Martin 2007), making it an important place for economic exchange.

Unlike the flow of capital, which crosses borders with few restrictions, the flow of people across this divide, specifically the mobility of working class women from Mexico to the United States, is severely limited. In 1993, the same year that NAFTA was enacted, the United States government became committed to deterring illegal immigration from Mexico (Cornelius 2007). The Border Patrol began a series of high-profile campaigns entitled "Operation Gatekeeper" in south San Diego and "Operation Hold-the-Line" in El Paso aimed at curbing illegal entries (Orrenius 2004; Andreas 2003). At this time, the main goals of the Border Patrol were to deter illegal immigration and illegal drugs from entering the U.S. (Andreas 2003).

The strategy that was used during this time was to increase enforcement at high traffic crossing areas by enhancing the number of Border Patrol agents guarding these areas. From September 1993 to September 2005, the number of Border Patrol agents rose from 3,965 to 11,106 and spending increased six times during this time period (Cornelius 2007: 2). Since the implementation of this aggressive border enforcement, the number of unauthorized immigrants in the United States has actually doubled (Passel 2006). As a result of the events of September 11th, border agencies "retooled and redesigned" the previous border strategy of drug enforcement and immigration to include counterterrorism in the enforcement apparatus (Andreas 2003: 1). Agencies now have greater responsibilities and high public expectations to deter immigration and protect the country's borders from further terrorist attacks. Inspections at the border became more thorough, which increased wait times at every major crossing. The budget for this enforcement also increased with an additional 2 billion dollars in 2003 (Andreas 2003: 7).

Technologically sophisticated surveillance equipment was also added along with fences and walls as a means to guard this divide (Cornelius 2007). These efforts did not curb illegal immigration attempts; instead they only moved the flow of migrants away from popular crossing points to more rugged and dangerous terrains (Massey, Durand, & Malone 2002, Cornelius 2001, Eschbach et al. 1999). The consequences of diverting the migrant stream has led to increased dangers for illegal migrants, many of who die on this journey.[4] In addition, this policy had the unintended consequence of extending the stay of both legal and illegal migrants whose migration was previously cyclical. Approximately 20 percent of migrants in 1992 returned home after six months, but by 2000 this number had dropped to 7 percent (Reyes, Johnson, and Swearingen 2002). The U.S.-Mexico border and its surrounding areas have been described as a "global crossroads" representing the social, economic, political, and cultural changes encountered across the world (Spener & Staudt 1998, 3). In the vast interdisciplinary borderlands literature, the notion of the border encompasses more than a physical international dividing line, but goes beyond this literal meaning to include metaphoric and affective meanings. The concept of "crossing borders" has been redefined as not geographic specific, but as representing borders that exist everywhere, which are fragmented and continually produced and crossed (Vila 2003). Gloria Anzaldua (1987), in her seminal book Borderlands/La Frontera, uses this term refer to the psychological, sexual, and spiritual spaces that are "present wherever two or more cultures edge each other, where people of different races occupy the same territory, where under, lower, middle, and upper classes touch, where the space between two individuals shrinks with intimacy" (19). These "border zones" are understood as areas that "become salient around such lines of sexual orientation, gender, class, race, ethnicity, nationality, age, politics, dress, food, and taste" (Rosaldo 1989, 207-8). The concept of borders has also been extended as a means to understand the formation of identities and the self. For

---

[4] Over 3,700 known migrant fatalities have been reported between the years 1995 and 2006 (Cornelius 2007).

example, Ruth Behar (1993) frames the construction of her own identity as an academic ethnographer based in the U.S. and that of her Mexican-based interviewee in relation to the borders that they both cross in the ethnographic encounter.

In this study, I approach the subject of "borders" as encompassing both the political barrier that separates nation states as well as the metaphoric boundaries that are created in these spaces. I borrow Kathleen Staudt and David Spener's (1998) explanation of the border as "an ongoing, dialectical process that generates multiple borderland spaces, some of which are not located very close to the official boundary itself" (4). Adopting this approach to the border and borderlands enables me to research and theorize women's subjective experiences in the multiple cross-border encounters they experience in their migration— between the United States and Mexico, between domestic workers and employers, and between "ethnic" Americans and "real" Americans. In other words, I seek to understand these experiences between gendered, classed, raced, and nationalized identities.

Conclusion

Despite the emergence of several recent studies on the movement of women workers across the world, the literature on women's migration, domestic labor, and transnationalism has not analyzed the temporary migration of women workers across national divides and the social and economic motivations that drive this form of migration. Furthermore, while interdisciplinary feminist scholarship has transformed the connotation of the term "borders" and "borderlands" to include the subjectivity of its inhabitants, they have also focused on US-based migrants who have access to means of self-representation. This scholarship is based on the subjective experiences of inhabiting the borderlands written by academic activists, who are primarily women of color. The subjects of my research are working class women from Mexico who do not have access to the spaces of these writers, nor do they have time to engage in these activities. This study addresses the shortcomings in the literature: first, by placing temporary migrants at the center of the analysis; and second, by focusing on working class women's experiences at the border and the subjectivities that are produced through inhabiting the borderlands into the archive of scholarship on migration. In doing so, this study will examine class, gender, and nationality in the placement of migrant women in domestic work. Additionally, this work will examine the structure of their labor, and the relationships between workers and employers by studying, for the first time, co-ethnic domestic workers and employers.

This study begins with a description of my fieldwork and data collection in Chapter 2. The topics and issues stated above begin to unfold in Chapter 3, where I examine the motivations for Mexican women's migration into the United States and highlight the differences between those women who immigrate and those who commute across borders. I also challenge the recent scholarship on Mexican women's migration, which depicts these women as passive actors in the migratory process, by examining cross-border workers determination to enter the United States to work in domestic service. To do this, I examine the financial stability of workers and their reliance on factory work in determining who is eligible to enter the United States legally. Finally, in this chapter, I analyze the topic of migrant women's empowerment which is a current debate in the migration literature. Since cross-border domestic workers are not setters, I examine this topic by asking: "Are women empowered by staying in Mexico? To answer this question, I analyze cross-border domestic workers' articulations of community and mobility in Mexico.

Chapter 4 follows with the exploration of the "transnational social spaces" cross-border domestic workers inhabit during their stay in the border city of Laredo and the multiple meanings of these spaces that workers, employers, and border officials occupy. I follow cross-border worker's journey to and from work and examine the shifts in their identities from consumers to producers in the "safe" and "risky" spaces they move through in this "border zone." I also examine how gender, class, and nationality expose women as undocumented workers in the different spaces they inhabit. In addition, I analyze the social networks across these transnational spaces and the centrality of cross-border workers in establishing cross-border linkages and producing these "deterritorialized" spaces.

Finally, in Chapter 5, I examine the occupation of domestic work in this border city and different jobs associated with this form of labor. I rely on the concept of symbolic boundaries to explore the inequalities of gender, class, and nationality between co-ethnic employers and domestic workers. I do this by examining employers' use of the material practice of food in their homes to communicate difference between themselves and their household workers. I also explore the production of ideal womanhood by domestic workers as a means to understand their identities as the "authentic" Mexican woman and to counter the indignities of class they experience daily at their workplace. Throughout the study, I intentionally shift the focus between the experiences of the cross-border domestic workers in Mexico and the United States so that both the reader and I also cross borders with these women.

CHAPTER 2

Listening to Border Women

Introduction

I met Letty Ochoa for the first time in the small house she shares with her husband. She invited me into her kitchen where we sat and chatted about her job with Yolanda, the employer she had been working with for over ten years.[5] As we sat at her kitchen table, she began showing me the different ingredients she uses in her cooking and how they differ from those her employer prefers her to use at work. She then began narrating a story about how she would sneak cubes of tomato flavoring from her home to her workplace in order to improve the taste of the rice she cooked for her employer and her employer's family. As we talked at length about her employer's food preferences, she thought it was necessary for me to taste her food myself, so I could understand why the ingredients she uses are so important. Over a plate of her enchiladas with a side of this special rice and a diet soda, we talked at length about work, family, and comida.

---

[5] To protect the cross-border domestic workers— both immigrant domestic workers and employers who participated— all of the names mentioned here are pseudonyms.

Ethnographic fieldwork and other forms of qualitative research are important methods for the study of domestic workers, who are typically reluctant to answer surveys or participate in formal interviews. The development of informal relations in these methods allows researchers to gain access into this community that is often hidden and inaccessible to outsiders. Scholars who study domestic service have relied heavily on different forms of qualitative methods to capture the experiences of domestic workers and their relationship with employers. Judith Rollins (1985) was one of the first scholars to conduct a qualitative study with women in this occupation. As a means to fully experience life as a maid, she herself worked in this occupation for over three months along with conducting interviews with African American domestic workers and white employers. Likewise, in her study on the three generations of Japanese domestic workers in the United States, Evelyn Glenn Nakano (1986) also employed qualitative methods through her long interviews with these different generations of workers. Mary Romero (1992) collected her data on twenty-five Chicana domestics by initiating "non-structured, free-flowing, and open-ended interviews to establish multiple identities and diffuse family and community roles" (7). Similarly, in her study on Mexican and Central American immigrant domestic workers, sociologist Pierrette Hondagneu-Sotelo (2001) also utilized in-depth open-ended interviews with maids and employers as well as collecting a non-random sampled survey with domestic workers waiting at bus stops. Along with interviewing Filipina domestic workers about the forms of labor control and discipline they experienced, Nicole Constable (1997) conducted participant-observation and observed workers' interactions with employers, their daily work routines, and also took part in their community activities and functions. Finally, in her recent book on domestic service in Taiwan, Pei-Chia Lan (2006) conducted long semi-structured interviews and participant observation with Taiwanese employers and Filipina and Indonesian domestic workers in an attempt to understand politics, race, ethnicity, and gender within workplace relationships.

I also utilized qualitative methods to study the "migration" of undocumented Mexican women domestic workers in border cities, their border-crossing experiences, and the inequalities of gender, class, and nationality. This chapter describes the methods I used to study cross-border domestic workers and employers, who opened their homes to me and gave me the privilege of witnessing and participating in their daily lives.

In December 2003, I entered the field for the first time as a researcher, where I conducted a pilot study with ten cross-border workers in Laredo, Texas. The goal of this study was to determine if Laredo/Nuevo Laredo border would be a good research site for this study and to get a feel for the type of data collection I would use for my study research. Since I grew up Laredo and since most my family continues to live in this city, I contacted these workers through family networks. Employers who I knew personally introduced me to the women who worked for them and from here I recruited a few of these workers' friends and relatives. From these initial interviews, I learned that although employer networks were useful in finding women for this study, my link to the employers adversely impacted my conversations with these working women. In one case in particular, I had contacted an

employer who invited me to her home to meet her
employee, Santa. When I met Santa at her employer's
house and told her about the study, she said that she would
be happy to participate. We agreed to meet at her house for
our conversation. During the interview, Santa was hesitant
to talk about her work experiences or anything in relation to
her employer and she actually seemed nervous when
talking about her work. I did not learn much from this
conversation and realized that I needed a different approach
in recruiting domestic workers for this study.

In January 2005, I re-entered the field and began my
data collection for this study at the Laredo, Texas and
Nuevo Laredo, Mexico border. Since I spent most of my
life Laredo, I was drawn to these cities as a research site for
this study. As a native Laredoan, I had the advantage of
being intimately familiar with everyday life in this border
town. For instance, I knew the popular bus stops that
domestic workers frequented and different neighborhoods
around town where a majority of these women are
employed. I was also familiar with the downtown of Nuevo
Laredo, which made crossing into this city alone less
intimidating. For these reasons, I was convinced that the
paired border cities of Laredo, Texas and Nuevo Laredo,
Mexico would be the perfect setting for this study.

The economy, history, and people of Laredo are
intimately linked with its "sister city," Nuevo Laredo,
Mexico, which is located across the Rio Grande river. The
city of Laredo has a population of over 200,000 residents
and is rated in the top 25 fastest growing cities in the
United States (U.S. Census Bureau 2006). With the growth
of the maquiladora industry in Nuevo Laredo and the
passage of the North American Free Trade Agreement,
Laredo has become the busiest inland port in the United

States. Despite this booming industry, Laredo continues to be ranked among the most impoverished cities in the United States, with the per capita income being $19,598 (U.S. Bureau of Economic Analysis 2006) and the average weekly wage being $477— almost half that of the state at $850 (Patrick 2007). Across the border in Nuevo Laredo, the economic conditions are far worse. The violent drug war in Nuevo Laredo, which became increasingly violent in 2005, has crippled the economy of this city (Thompson 2005a; Thompson 2005b). Tourism, which remains an important source of revenue for this city, has dwindled as a consequence. The cross-border traffic at this port of entry is one of the busiest in the nation. Research on cross-border movement has identified Laredo as having the highest number of women crossing legally on a frequent basis of all land ports between the U.S. and Mexico (Alegria 2002).

In order to understand the temporary migration of Mexican women workers and their experiences in domestic service, I included two samples of domestic workers for this study: cross-border domestics (those who live in Nuevo Laredo and work in Laredo) and immigrant domestic workers (who live in Laredo and work in Laredo). A total of twenty-six cross-border domestic workers were interviewed. I made an effort to recruit a diverse sample of domestic workers by including women across age groups, day workers and partial live-ins, and women who held various levels of experience within the occupation. I also considered the type of work they did, interviewing women experienced in all the different forms of domestic labor. In the next chapter, I discuss the specific demographics of these women workers. In order to gain a better understanding of cross-border laborers and the occupation of domestic service in this border town, I included nine immigrant workers in this sample. In addition, I interviewed five ex-domestic workers (three cross-border and two immigrant) in order to gain a sense of what motivates some women to abandon this line of work, as well as three government-sponsored caretakers for the elderly, locally referred to as palomitas, as a means to understand other work options available to migrant women workers.[6]

Fifteen employers were interviewed for this study. All of the employers had lived in Laredo most of their lives and identified themselves as having Mexican ancestry. The average age of employers was 43, with the youngest being 25 and the oldest 65 years old. All of the employers had previous experience hiring domestic workers in the past. Many employers grew up with maids in their homes and had employed domestic help all of their adult lives. The employers in this sample were highly educated, with only three of the employers having not completed college. All but one of these women was married, and most had children. Four employers were housewives or retired, nine worked full time, and one worked part-time. In addition to these interviews, I also interviewed community members on their perspectives on Mexican cross-border domestic workers in the city; these included a city council member, social service workers, and a downtown Laredo merchant.

---

[6] The *palomitas* were an interesting addition to the sample in that it revealed the work options for women who could legally work, yet spoke little to no English. Two of these three women worked as domestic workers before they became legal residents. In one case the *palomita* was also a cross-border worker, but was crossing and working legally using her legal residence status.

After my initial experience with using employer contacts to recruit domestic workers in my pilot study, I decided to cut employer ties with my domestic work sample by recruiting domestic workers using snowball sampling through domestic worker networks. This was more difficult than I had originally expected. I quickly discovered that the domestic worker population existed in an entirely different world that was unavailable to me. To gain entry into this world, I began visiting bus stops around the city during different hours of the day for the purpose of meeting these women, finding that the best times to talk to domestic workers were at the main bus stop between 7:30-9:00am, and at neighborhood bus stops between 3:30-5:00pm while they were waiting for busses to take them back to the downtown. Afternoons were the best times to talk to these women since these busses were often late, forcing domestic workers to wait for their ride to the downtown area. The first two months in the field were spent trying to recruit women for the study at these bus stops around town. Since the majority of cross-border domestic workers are unauthorized workers, many women were cautious about even talking to me at these bus stops. After several unsuccessful attempts, I made the decision to hire a research assistant to help with recruiting. Through my sister, I hired a local college student to accompany me in the recruiting and in traveling to Nuevo Laredo for interviews. She was outgoing and was also a Nuevo Laredo resident. When the two of us began frequenting bus stops, we were able to sell this study as a "student project" and were able to convince a few women to participate. Through these participants, I was able to use snowball sampling to recruit their friends and family members who were also domestic workers.

One problem with this form of recruitment was that I was only introduced to the population of cross-border domestics and not immigrant domestic workers. The population of immigrant domestics was extremely difficult to locate and recruit since most live with their employers and do not congregate at bus stops like the cross-border population. Of those immigrant workers who lived outside of their employer's homes, most either drove to their workplace or were given rides by family members. Due to the difficulty of locating this population, I resorted to using employer contacts to recruit immigrant women for my study. Since this group of women is not at the center of the study, I was satisfied with the number of interviewees whom I was able to contact. As an incentive, I offered $20.00 to all participants in this study. Although this money could not adequately compensate them form the risks that they took by talking with a stranger, the women seemed eager to share their experiences with me and seemed to enjoy narrating their life stories.

All employers were contacted using social networks with community members. Most employers were happy to participate in the study and were readily available. For this group, I again utilized snowball sampling. I sought out a diverse sample by including employers of nannies, housekeepers, and healthcare workers. I also sampled to include employers of different ages and experiences. Additionally, I made an attempt to include employers from different neighborhoods across the city in order to capture diverse class statuses.

In order to capture the rich and detailed experiences of the domestic workers and employers in this study, I relied on the qualitative technique of long semi-structured interviews for my conversations with domestic workers and employers. In qualitative research, interviews are guided conversations that allow the researcher to explore the details of people's experiences and their views on reality to generate theory (Reinharz 1992). The interviewee is the center of the conversation and topics of inquiry are guided by both the researcher and the participant. Detailed descriptions of the meanings people attribute to their social actions emerge from these interviews (Weiss 1994). Long in-depth interviews become ethnographic when the main goal is not "studying people" but instead "learning from people" (Spradley 1979: 3).

In order to gain a better sense of the life experiences of the domestic workers in this study, I made an effort to interview both immigrant domestic workers and cross-border domestic workers in their homes. Most women preferred holding these conversations in their homes instead of in public spaces. In a few cases, the interviews took place at a friend's house, who had also been interviewed for the study. Two of the interviews with cross-border domestics were conducted in public areas: a public park in Nuevo Laredo and in a restaurant in the downtown Laredo. Most interviews took place inside participants' living rooms, kitchens, or bedrooms, with few outside on the patio. The setting of the home was important since it gave me a feel for the family life of these women workers. I often met family members, friends, and neighbors during my visits. Although conversing with these women in their houses greatly enhanced my understanding of their domestic situation and their neighborhood localities, and therefore of their lives outside of work, their homes were not always the best places for interviews. Many conversations were cut short by friends stopping by to visit or by husbands or family members returning home from work. For example, when I had met with Rosie Sanchez, we were sitting outside on her driveway chatting when her friend Daniela Cruz, whom I had previously interviewed, showed up to visit with Rosie. The topic of our conversation quickly switched from domestic labor to Rosie's upcoming baby shower. After chatting for a while, I decided to continue with our interview some other day. During these interviews, I often had an audience of children and spouses, who sat around the table while their mother/wife was telling her story, which may have influenced their responses to some of my questions. For example, in one interview, the respondent, my assistant, and I sat in her living room while her husband was resting in the bedroom after his night shift at a local factory. When she was describing how her husband was not happy about her working in Laredo, she began whispering, worried that he might be listening through the door.

Interviews with immigrant women living with their employers took place in their employer's homes; these included three caretakers of elderly women and one nanny. Since I was introduced to the caretakers of the elderly through their employers, it was their employers who invited me to the homes of their elderly parents to talk to the domestic workers. Employers were not present for these interviews— only the domestics while their "patients" remained in the room. During these interviews, I was able to witness first-hand their duties and the kind of care they gave to their patients. At one house, two sisters were caring for an elderly woman in a vegetative state. As we were talking, the bedridden woman began coughing violently.

The caretakers jumped up, cleared her throat, and placed the respirator over the woman's nose. While I watched with amazement at their ease of handling the needs of this woman, they continued chatting with me as if nothing had just happened. In the case of the one live-in nanny I interviewed, I was introduced to her through an immigrant domestic in the sample. I had no idea when this interview would take place, only that I would receive a phone call from the worker. When I was called, the domestic worker asked me to meet her at her employer's house. As we spoke, she was caring for a three-month-old baby, which she held in her arms throughout the entire interview.

Interviews with employers took place at their workplace or in their homes, when the domestic worker was not present. Unlike the domestic work sample, on very few occasions did I meet employers' family members and friends. Most employers were very comfortable with being interviewed and talked to me candidly about their experiences with this occupation. The length of these interviews was shorter than those with domestics, with the average lasting only one hour.

Before I could begin interviewing, I had to figure out how to safely travel to Nuevo Laredo. Due to the ongoing drug war, shootings, kidnappings, and slayings were an almost daily occurrence on this side of the border. When I entered the field, I knew that I had to take precautions, but at the same time I did not want this violence to interfere with the quality of the interviews. I wanted to follow my plan of conducting interviews in the setting where domestics were most comfortable, which meant I had to spend a large portion of my time in Nuevo Laredo. As I mentioned before, I recruited a local student to accompany me to my interviews in Nuevo Laredo. She was a Nuevo Laredo resident and was familiar with the different neighborhoods across town. In the beginning, this arrangement worked out perfectly, but as her student workload began to increase, my time in the field subsequently decreased. The violence in Nuevo Laredo was discomforting, so I had to find another assistant. In order to continue with my research, I hired a cross-border domestic worker who had participated in my pilot study and whom I had re-contacted for a follow-up interview. Since she owned a car and only worked on Mondays and Thursdays, this arrangement was ideal. She took me to all of my scheduled interviews and she introduced me to her friends who were also cross-border domestic workers. Each time I traveled to an interview, I would park my car on the Laredo side of the border and cross on foot into Nuevo Laredo where I would meet my research assistant. By walking back and forth across the border, I often crossed alongside women whom I suspected were domestic workers coming home from work. I also witnessed the process of border-crossing into the United States on my return travels to Laredo.

Scheduling the interviews with domestic workers was another challenge in the data collection process. I quickly learned that these women are extremely busy and finding a time for an interview would prove difficult. Most women did not return to their homes until the evenings and often worked six days of the week. I had to schedule interviews either in the late evenings or during the few hours they had free on their days off. Contacting women to schedule an interview also was a challenge. While some women had phones in their houses, many did not and instead would give me the phone number of a family member or a neighbor. In one case, a cross-border domestic worker gave me the phone number of her sister who lived down the street from her. When I called the number, a child answered the phone and ran down the street to call her aunt to the phone. Unfortunately for myself and the little girl, who went through the trouble of running down the street, her aunt was not home and so I had to try again at another time. Often messages I left for workers were simply never received or returned. In several cases, I had to make multiple trips to the home of the respondent just to make contact with her. In the case of one cross-border domestic worker, I had to visit her house four times before I finally found her at home by showing up late in the evening.

The interviews with domestic workers were typically long. They ranged from forty-five minutes to four hours, with most interviews lasting approximately two hours in length. All of the interviews were recorded with the consent of the respondent. I used a portable digital voice recorder with a lapel microphone to capture the conversations I had with these participants. Although a few people seemed nervous when the recorder was first switched on, once the conversation began most participants seemed to forget it was in place.

In my interviews with domestic workers, I sought to understand their migratory experiences, motivations for entering this occupation, the duties and expectations at their workplace, and life on the borderlands. Employers were asked about their history of hiring domestics, experiences with current and past employees, and domestic work on the border.

After each interview, I wrote lengthy fieldnotes of all my observations. Many times, I dictated these notes on my recorder between interviews, while other times I rushed to my car to jot down everything I could remember; details included a description of the respondent's appearance, expressions, and demeanor. I also recorded descriptions of their house, family members present, and any other details that might have drawn my attention. In total, I collected forty-six interviews in Spanish and twenty interviews in English. As the interviews became more numerous, I realized that I could not keep up with the transcription. Spanish transcription was especially difficult since I am much more comfortable with written English. I hired a native Spanish speaker to transcribe all of the interviews that were conducted in Spanish. I transcribed a majority of the English interviews myself and hired a transcriber when this work became too overwhelming.

I began the analysis of this study while I was still in the field collecting data. In the fieldnotes I wrote after each interview, I recorded the themes and patterns I identified as emerging from each conversation. Additionally, writing and reflecting immediately after each interview forced me to rethink the interview questions and refine these questions for subsequent interviews as I went along. I cleaned each of the interview transcripts, which involved listening to the recorded interviews and correcting all errors. Once this was finished, I used the qualitative software, NVIVO, to code all interviews, fieldnotes, and memos. I began by using "open coding," which entails reading through the materials and identifying initial categories and analytic concepts in this data. This is an inductive approach where concepts and insights are identified and developed instead of using pre-established categories and fitting these to the data. I wrote memos of the different categories that were emerging and then analyzed the materials again, using "focused coding," which involves carefully reading data while building on the main themes and categories that were established (Emerson, Fretz, & Shaw 1995). From this analysis, I was able to piece together thematic narratives and write chapter outlines for this study.

As I mentioned earlier, I spent my childhood and most of my young adult life in Laredo, Texas. In choosing this research site, I hoped that my background in Laredo would give me an advantage upon entering the field and in my interactions with Mexican women and Mexican American employers. However, like other researchers, I too was challenged with my status as both an "insider" and "outsider" in both communities. Insider research, which describes scholars studying their own communities or society, has long been debated among anthropologists and sociologists. Proponents of insider research argue that this research allows for more open dialogue with subjects, ease of entry into the field, improved ability to blend into situations, and additional verbal and non-verbal advantages (Aguilar 1981). Critics state that these researchers are at a disadvantage in that due to their familiarity with the community, important questions are overlooked, the outcome of findings are subject to researcher bias, and participants may see the researcher as a threat and, consequently, might withhold information (Ibid). This debate has moved beyond these differences, especially in feminist scholarship where the terms "insider" and "outsider" are considered essentializing, by not recognizing the complicated and multilayered identities of researchers and communities (Robinson 1994; Lal 1998; Nagar 1997; Vo 2000). Rather than having fixed identities, researchers are considered as belonging to a "scholarship of the world" and, therefore, can move across communities (Narayan 1993). In relation to my own experience in the field, my position as an insider and outsider was blurred in some circumstances but, in others, made abundantly clear.

I had no illusions about fitting in with the domestic worker population. Even though I am from Laredo, my own middle-class community seemed like a world apart from that of the women working in domestic service (Lal 1998, Collins 1986, Zavella 1992). First, these women live in Nuevo Laredo and although they reside only across the border from Laredo, the differences in lifestyle are vast. Second, when I began my fieldwork, my fluency in Spanish was rusty at best. My initial struggles with the language set me apart from domestic workers, who speak little to no English. When I entered the field and began interacting with these women, I realized immediately that these differences spanned beyond nativity and language to class. The main marker of my "outsider" status was my position as a researcher, which they understood essentially as my belonging to a privileged class. Most women could not understand why I was conducting this research at all and wondered how I could spend all of my time out in the field instead of working a "real" job. For example, in the middle of an interview with Alicia Navarro, who was my age and had been working since she was in her teens, when she was explaining her recent financial hardships and struggles as a single mother, she began asking me questions about my personal life. She wanted to know why I was in school for so long, if I had ever worked, and if I was married or had any children. At the time, I was unmarried with no children and had a very short employment history. From that point, I realized that she was communicating to me that, with my background, I could not relate to her experiences. Also, before entering into their homes, many women made a point to tell me that their house was very humble, nothing like the houses they had been to in Laredo.

During our conversations, domestic workers saw me as someone from Laredo and associated me as being part of the employer class. After the interviews were over, women regularly asked me if I knew someone who was looking for household help. I was asked if I myself needed some help with cleaning or if my mother needed assistance around the house. Even after several interactions, women still looked to me as a possible entry into the employer network. Domestic workers viewed me as a stranger to their community, but also as a possible professional resource. These interactions gave me a sense of the precarious nature of their occupation, in which women were constantly searching for contacts for future employment, in case their employer fired them or were looking for a replacement job with an employer they were unhappy with.

My interactions and conversations with employers were very different from those with domestic workers. Before returning to Laredo for this project, I would visit the city during holidays or long breaks, but I had not been a part of this community since I moved away from Laredo almost ten years before. Patricia Zavella (1992) explores the dilemma of balancing being positioned as a "cultural insider" and a Chicana feminist during fieldwork within her own community.[7] Some employers viewed me as part of the employer group and talked about their employees as if they were chatting with a friend. With other employers in

---

[7] See also Lal (1998) and Zavella (1992).

the sample, living away from Laredo (and specifically away from Texas), and being in the researcher position, disrupted my claim to being an "insider." Employers themselves communicated to me that I was no longer part of the Laredo community. For instance, during our interviews, many employers translated common Spanish phrases for me, which is uncommon in discourse among fellow Laredoans. Also, many employers in our conversations would explain local events and customs, as if I were a newcomer in the community. The boundaries in the relationships between researchers and co-ethnic subjects are often difficult to maintain (Vo 2000). In some of my interactions with employers, these boundaries were established through their subtle communication of our differences.

At the start of this chapter, I began with a description of one of my conversations with Letty Ochoa, a cross-border domestic worker. This description reveals the typical structure of the conversations I had with most of the women in this study. As a researcher, I had the idea that I was going to talk with these women about migration and domestic work, and instead the participants in this study often took charge of the conversation themselves, bringing in topics that they believed were important in understanding their experiences as workers, such as Letty on the topic of food. This approach allowed for a deeper understanding of the different experiences of being a border crosser and an undocumented worker along with a better understanding of the multiple dimensions of their lives. The following chapters of this study build on the major findings that emerged from these conversations with these brave women who welcomed me into their homes and graciously shared their stories.

CHAPTER 3
Becoming a Cross-Border Worker

Introduction

When Lucia Hernandez was a teenager, she and her sisters traveled from San Luis Potosi and paid a coyote (a guide) to sneak them across the Nuevo Laredo/Laredo border. After successfully crossing the border, Luisa found a job as an undocumented live-in maid and stayed at this job for five years in Laredo. One evening, after leaving church, she was apprehended by the border patrol, questioned, and was quickly sent back to Nuevo Laredo. Instead of returning to San Luis Potosi, she and a few of her sisters decided to settle in Nuevo Laredo where there was a chance of finding work in a factory. Fifteen years later, Lucia was again working in Laredo as a domestic worker, but this time she was a legal border crosser who returns to her own house after work, where she lived with her two young sons in Nuevo Laredo.

In the last thirty years, migrants from Mexico have entered the United States in unprecedented numbers, dramatically transforming the profile of the United States. Since 1980, foreign–born Mexicans residing in the United States has increased from 2.2 million to the 2006 estimate of 11.5 million. Among these migrants, 6.6 million are unauthorized to reside or work in the United States (Batalova 2008). The number of Mexican women migrants entering the United States has also increased from 1980, where 300,000 undocumented women were reported as entering the United States, to 1.1 million between 2001 and 2006 (Fry 2006). The three states with the highest population of Mexican workers, California, Texas, and Illinois, continue to receive most of the incoming migrants, yet the numbers of incoming migrants to these major states has been declining since 1990 (Durand et al. 2001). Many major cities in these states are saturated with unskilled migrant labor, thus potential migrants are shifting to non-traditional points of destination in search of better employment opportunities and higher wages. States that have historically had low numbers of Mexican migrants, such as South Dakota, Louisiana, Alaska, and Ohio, have doubled in this population between 2000 and 2006 (Fry 2006). Mexican women migrants are fast becoming an important segment of these non-traditional destinations as well.

The topic of documented and undocumented Mexican migration has been extensively studied by sociologists and migration scholars. Until recently, the movement of this population was centered on the experiences of men migrating for the purpose of employment, while often ignoring the migration of Mexican women (Koussoujji and Ranni 1984). Like men, women are typically introduced to the idea of migration through a family member or a parent (Cerrutti & Massey 2001), and are especially likely to leave Mexico for the United States when an immediate family member is a migrant in the destination country (Donato 1993). Yet, unlike men who often migrate without their spouses, women's migration usually begins by following a male relative rather than initiating this movement themselves (Cerrutti & Massey 2001). Most studies on Mexican women's migration focus on long-term migratory experiences with an emphasis on settlement (Hondagneu-Sotelo 1994). Scholars have noted that the migratory experience is felt not only by those making the journey, but also by those persons who are left behind (Bever 2002; Aysa and Massey 2004). To date, very little is known about the motivations and experiences of women who temporarily enter into the U.S. for labor.

In this chapter, I begin by examining the multiple factors that have contributed to Mexican women's migration into the United States. I explore the policies that have influenced the migration of these women, the socio-economic conditions that motivated them to leave Mexico, the demand for their labor, and the more individual explanations at the personal level for their migrations. I later examine the process of becoming a cross-border domestic worker, and argue that, unlike long-term immigrants, working as temporary cross-border domestic workers provides women with the opportunity to initiate their movement across the border and enter the U.S. for the purpose of labor. Following this, I explore the advantages and disadvantages of staying in Mexico as opposed to immigrating for settlement in the United States. I argue that the examination of cross-border workers sheds light on Mexican women's motivations, decisions, and participation in labor migration, which is often otherwise overlooked in the examination of long-term migration.

Motivations for Women's Migration

Mexican immigration has historically been a male-dominated movement. The first major policy related to Mexican migration was the Bracero Program that began in 1942 and was later eliminated in 1964. This program, which began as a means to address the labor shortages of WWII, brought Mexican laborers to work primarily in agriculture with temporary visas. It is estimated that hundreds of thousands of primarily male Mexican workers participated in this program (Craig 1971). This temporary labor created an "elastic supply of labor" which met the labor needs of the seasonal agricultural industries and eased the labor demands in Mexico (Hondagneu-Sotelo 1994). When this program was terminated in 1964, the demand for Mexican agricultural labor continued, and workers who had entered the U.S. legally under the Bracero Program continued to seek employment in the United States. What is referred to as the "modern era" of Mexico-U.S. migration begins with the termination of this program in which Mexican workers continued to seek employment in the U.S. with and without legal documentation (Cerrutti & Massey 2004).

Pirrette Hondagneu-Sotlo (1994) contends that the current flow of Mexican women into the United States began with the Bracero Program. One year after this program was terminated, what is considered one of the most important immigration policies in the United States, the Hart-Keller Act of 1965, was enacted. This legislation replaced the discriminatory quota system that was in place since 1920, which banned African and Asian immigration and limited the entry of Southern and Eastern Europeans. Instead, each country in Europe, Asia, Africa, and the Pacific were given 20,000 visas per year. These quotas did not apply for immigrants from Mexico and other Latin American countries, furthering the growth of Mexican emigration (Craig 1971). The legal immigration of Mexican immigrants became more difficult under later amendments established in 1968. Once legal entry was restricted, unauthorized immigration dramatically increased. In year 1964, Border officials apprehended and deported 87,000 undocumented Mexican migrants, yet by 1986, this number escalated to the apprehension of 1.8 million (Cornelius 1992). The combination of the dramatic increase in illegal immigration and the economic difficulties that the U.S. was experiencing at the time made immigration a priority on the political agenda of the public (Massey 1999), and resulted in the Immigration and Reform Act of 1986 (IRCA), which was the first legislation aimed at curbing illegal immigration. This policy enacted several provisions to control illegal immigration: (1) for the first time, sanctions against employers who knowingly hired illegal workers were enacted; (2) funding for the Border Patrol was increased for the purpose of deterring immigrants from entering the U.S. – an estimated 400 million dollars was allocated for this enforcement (Bean et al 1989); (3) Mexicans who had been living in the U.S. without documentation before 1982 and persons who could prove they were employed in agriculture for at least 90 days were offered amnesty. Offering amnesty in this policy was an attempt to "wipe the slate clean" and to appease the Latino civil rights groups (Cerrutti and Massey 2004). Under this provision, 2.3 million Mexicans were given temporary residence (ibid).

One of the unintended consequences of this policy was that after IRCA was enacted, women began emigrating

both legally and illegally into the U.S. in unprecedented
numbers (Durand et al 1999; Cornelius 1992). Across the
Mexican community, there was a fear that this policy
would "close the door" on the movement of Mexican
immigrants, which at the time was often seasonal and
temporary (Cornelius 1992, 179). Women began leaving
Mexico to join their husbands in the hopes that they too
would become legalized (Cornelius 1992). This policy
created a wave of family reunification among the Mexicans
in which close family members left Mexico to join their
legalized relatives. Before the enactment of IRCA, women
were estimated as comprising one fourth of the
undocumented Mexican migrant population; this rose to
one third after the implementation of this policy (Massey et
al. 2002).   Once again, an unintended consequence of
'Operation Gatekeeper' in 1993, which enhanced border
enforcement as a means to deter illegal immigration, was
what scholars have referred to as the "feminization of
migration" (ibid). Mexican male immigrants began
extending the duration of their trips in fear that they would
not be able to safely return to the U.S. As a result, these
immigrants called for their families to join them in the
U.S., creating an influx of women's migrants. While the
U.S. is now making it harder for Mexican migrants to enter
the U.S., the demand for this labor continues, especially for
women migrants, whose work in domestic service is
necessary for the caretaking of American dual-career
families in need of inexpensive labor. Scholars have found
that an increase in the U.S. employment growth is followed
by the likelihood of illegal migration (Massey and Espinosa
1997).

The Mexican economy has also driven Mexican women
and men from their homes in Mexico to seek better lives in

the United States. Between 1965 and 1982, the Mexican economy rapidly expanded with large-scale investment in internal markets, creating national growth in production (Hansen 1971); this period is also referred to as the "oil boom" in Mexico, yet when the petroleum supplies around the world began to rise, the price in oil plummeted, resulting in an economic crisis in Mexico in 1982. (Sheahan 1991), as a result of which the peso lost value. During the time of the enactment of IRCA, the Mexican economy collapsed, and the Mexican government followed a stabilization strategy dictated by the International Monetary Fund. The IMF package included a call for reducing public spending, raising public sector prices, and removing barriers to imports (Loaeza 2006). As a consequence, Mexicans of all classes experienced dramatic declines in both their wages and opportunities for employment within the formal sector. Urban wages dropped by 47 percent and almost a third of the population was earning less than twice the minimum wage (Sheahan 1991). These difficult economic conditions forced individuals to consider migration as a strategy for survival (Gonzalez de la Rocha 1993). Another result of the downward turn of the Mexican economy was that the sole income of a male breadwinner was no longer financially sufficient to sustain many families. The growing numbers of foreign factories that have relocated into Mexico have also transformed local economies, bringing women closer to the U.S.-Mexico border, and making emigration to the United States a logical alternative to industrial work (Tiano 1994). As a consequence, both married and single women, who previously would not have entered the workforce, were driven to find employment in order to help support their families (Gonzalez de la Rocha 1993).

However, poverty, lack of viable employment, and immigration policies do not sufficiently explain the migration of Mexican women into the United States. Pierrette Hondagneu-Sotelo (1994) argues that gendered relations in the household must also be considered when attempting to understand the process of both men and women's migration. She finds that patriarchy within Mexican homes impacts the migration of women and men differently. Gendered relations in the home encourage men to migrate alone, which may or may not lead to settlement, while women respond to these patriarchal constraints by migrating for permanent settlement. Once women began migrating in larger numbers, they established a distinct set of women-centered networks, which facilitated the entry of even more women into the U.S. (ibid). These social networks are often family-centered (Mines and Massey 1985), and are found to be more important for women than for men in that these social connections serve as forms of protection for future women migrants, and consequently encourage further emigration into the United States (Massey and Espinosa 1997). Although these social networks facilitate their movement, women's migration varies by community and by personal experiences. Women sometimes choose to migrate in order to escape a violent marriage or the clutches of their parents (Hirsch 2002), thus reinforcing the view that the migration of Mexican women involves both macro economic and political influences, as well as the gendered experiences in the home (Hondagneu-Sotleo 1994).

Unlike their immigrant counterparts who enter the U.S. primarily for family reunification and look for employment later, the primary purpose for the entry of cross-border domestic workers is for labor. The motivations for this labor "migration" of cross-border workers are intimately linked to economic necessity, which differ from immigrant women whose primary goal is to ultimately settle in the U.S. In the next section, I describe the demographics of this group of women and how their socioeconomic positions influence their decisions to seek employment outside of Mexico.

The Profile of a Cross-Border Worker

The average age of the cross-border workers in this study was 39 years old, with the youngest woman being 23 and the oldest 86. The majority of the women (80 percent) were married or in a civil union, and all but two of these women had children. Most of women had small families of less than five household members, and only four women had more than three children. The majority of these women (66 percent) had been born in central Mexico and migrated to Nuevo Laredo with their parents, husbands, or as young adults in search of employment. One illustration of this pattern was Lucia Hernandez, who left her rural community in San Luis Potosi as a teenager for a better life in Nuevo Laredo. She and her sisters were drawn to Nuevo Laredo by an aunt who had recently taken residence in this city.

> I was motivated to leave. As a little girl, I began thinking about how one day I was going to leave this ranch. Even at such a young age, I didn't like ranch life—more than that, I detested it. I don't know if it was poverty that made me feel this way, but I would say to myself that one day I was going

to leave and never come back; that when I get older, I'd go to find a better life for myself. I didn't want to be buried there. I didn't want to meet my husband there. There is no future there; you can't earn enough to eat. I have always aspired for something better, for me and for my family. And now that we are here, it's like something has been lifted and I feel as if I can breathe.

For many of the cross-border domestic workers who were not native to Nuevo Laredo, the city offered employment opportunities that were unavailable in their small communities, along with the added benefit of schooling for their children. Despite these increased employment opportunities, many women struggled to find viable employment in this border city.

The low educational levels of the women in this sample limited their employment options in Mexico. Half the women in this study had a sixth grade education or less, and those few who had finished high school or had studied a trade did not work in the field they were trained for. The majority of the women in this study were employed in Nuevo Laredo before seeking work on the U.S. side of the border. Many women had been working as domestic workers in Nuevo Laredo (27%), earning about $15 a day less than they did in Laredo, though they worked longer hours. Three women had been employed in Laredo as live-in domestics in their teens and returned to get married or to rejoin their families in Mexico. A few women had been self-employed by selling tamales, tacos, or costume jewelry from their homes. The most common past occupation, however, was factory work, with almost half of these women (43%) having had previous experience in this line of employment. The minimum wage for a factory worker in Nuevo Laredo is 0.95 cents per hour (Laredo Development Foundation 2005), and the daily minimum wage is about $4.00 for urban workers and about $3.50 for rural workers (Pisani and Yoskowitz 2001, p. 71). In their study on the supply and demand of Mexican maids in Laredo, economists Michael J. Pisani and David Yoskowitz found that day maids (both cross-border workers and immigrant) earned $3.44 an hour and live-in maids earned $2.61[8] (2001: 79). In factory work across most developing countries, women are easily laid off during times of recession, and are paid only 50 to 60 percent of men's earnings for similar work (Bulbeck 1998, 176). Among the women I interviewed, a few had been laid off as the result of their factory closing or an oversupply of workers, but most women left factory work on their own accord to engage in domestic work where wages are significantly higher and which offered a more flexible schedule.

The typical wage for a live-out domestic worker in Laredo was between 30 to 35 dollars a day (I discuss wages for different domestic jobs in more detail in Chapter 5). By crossing into Laredo, Mexican women working full-time in domestic service can earn more than triple their previous income in factory work or in other occupations. Carolina Alvarez, a thirty-year-old mother of two small children, struggled with her decision to leave her previous

---

[8] In this study, the authors collected 195 non-random sampled surveys with domestic workers and 195 non-random sampled surveys with employers in Laredo, Texas. They found that their employers sample quoted slightly higher wages than the employee sample.

occupation to work in domestic service. When I asked her if she liked her new job in Laredo, she said:

> No one likes working as a house cleaner because it's basically the same thing that you do in your own home. I used to work as a secretary [for three years] and I would say that I would never go to that side [Laredo] to work, that I would always work in a job that I liked; but this couldn't be, because what I earned here [in Nuevo Laredo] working a full week, I can make on the other side in two days.

Cross-border domestic workers who worked full-time were the primary income providers in their homes. Most husbands were employed full-time as either factory workers or as day laborers. Two husbands were unemployed due and injury or illness, and two others were looking for employment. Those women who were married to factory workers had several advantages over other women as many factories helped their workers, who otherwise would not have the financial means, buy homes across the city and also provided health insurance for families.   Additionally, unlike day work or self-employment, factory work provided steady pay. In traditional Mexican culture, patriarchal ideologies dictate that the man of the house is the primary wage-earner, and that he alone should provide for his wife and children. But in contemporary Mexico, where wages are low and viable employment is scarce for those persons in skilled and unskilled labor, families struggle to live on a single-wage, thus driving women into the labor force in large numbers.

In the case of the families of these cross-border domestic workers, the combination of their American wages and their husbands' earnings do not provide luxuries, but allows them to own modest homes, send their children to school, and provide the basic living necessities for their families. In many cases, the modest wages these workers earned supported their immediate families in Nuevo Laredo and their grown children, as was the case with Juanita Gonzales. She was a sixty-two year old cross-border domestic worker, who has been working in Laredo for over forty years to support her six children. At the time of the interview she was financially assisting two of her older sons and their families.

> The money goes farther when I work on that side [Laredo]. For example, my son, who lives behind my house, works a print shop here in Nuevo Laredo, and he earns $1,200 pesos [approximately $116] a week. What can you do with 1,200 pesos when you have three people to support? He does not pay rent because he lives on my lot. I help him out with what I can, like when I go buy groceries, I also pick some up for him. They do not ask me, but if I hear that my granddaughter needs new shoes or a new school uniform, I go right away to the store and put it on layaway, so by wintertime she has what she needs. Those are the expenses that I help out with because I know that what he earns is not enough.

Despite suffering with arthritis in her knees, she continues to work three times a week to support her husband and help out her family. Since she works in Laredo, where wages are higher compared to similar work in Nuevo Laredo, Juanita has the extra income to help her children with their expenses.

Becoming a Border Crosser

Studies have found that is not the very poor in Mexico who enter the U.S., but those who have the economic means to pay for their passage into the U.S. (Cerrutti and Massey 2004); this also applies to cross-border domestic workers. Only a certain population of women has a chance at obtaining a border-crossing visa to enter Laredo temporarily and possibly earn the comparably higher wages that domestic work in this city provides. In order to cross the border using a border-crossing visa, Mexican residents must apply for this visa at the American consulate. All applicants are interviewed and must pay a $100 non-refundable application fee. To be eligible, the following criteria must be met: "Applicants must demonstrate that they have ties to Mexico that would compel them to return after a temporary stay in the United States. U.S. consular officers look for evidence of strong family, business, or social ties" (United States Department of State 2002). In other words, the applicant must convince consulate officers that they have a good reason for temporary travel across this divide (Brezosky 2006). In addition to these requirements, applicants must have a valid Mexican passport, present proof of "economic solvency," and show documentation of employment in Mexico (Ramirez 2001).

These requirements facilitate the passage of border crossers who can demonstrate they have the economic means to shop and visit within the U.S. border cities, and exclude those who do not have financial resources for these activities. Proving financial resources and economic stability were the most challenging tasks for a majority of these women. The women in this study brought to their consulate interviews letters from employers, bank statements, proof of homeownership and other documents to improve their chances of qualifying for this visa. Older workers and women who were native to Nuevo Laredo had an advantage over newcomers from the interior of Mexico in that they were more likely to be homeowners with longstanding bank accounts in Nuevo Laredo. Many long-time Nuevo Laredo residents have the additional advantage of having qualified for this visa in the years before 2001, when the requirements were less stringent. Their longstanding crossing record demonstrated to officers that they were likely to continue residing in Nuevo Laredo and not use this visa for long-term migration into the United States. But even for those women who had been crossing for many years, upon renewal of their visa in 2001, they too had to prove employment in Mexico or economic support if asked.[9] For many cross-border domestics, proving employment is a difficult hurdle in the renewal process. Domestics cannot reveal their income generated by their employment in domestic service in Laredo since it is unauthorized. Women who were married to factory workers applied as their husband's dependents. Those women whose husbands worked in the informal labor market in Nuevo Laredo did not have the necessary employment

---

[9] In the year 2001, as a means to tighten border crossing, the U.S. Department of State issued a new biometric laser visa which imposed new restrictions on travel and for the first time an expiration date on these border crossing visas (U.S. Department of State 2002). In then next chapter I discuss the details of this border crossing visa and the means by which women become eligible for this card.

documentation to prove employment to consulate officials and had to be resourceful when submitting their application. For example, Juanita Gonzales earned more than her husband who was retired and worked as a part-time repairman. When it came time to renew her visa, because she could not document her own undocumented employment in Laredo, she depended on family members for proof of support. Although in reality, it was Juanita and her husband who owned the home that her son was living in and it was her earnings that financially supported her son and his family, when she applied for a visa, she creatively inverted their domestic situation.

> When they started requiring the laser visa, we had to [renew our visas]. We had some problems because now they are asking that you to show you have money in the bank, who supports you, and explain why you want it. But since my son has a job in Nuevo Laredo, he presented papers for me saying that he was supporting me and that I lived with him, and with that I got it.

Since cross-border domestic workers could not prove their undocumented earnings in the U.S. as a household wage, they instead relied on the assumption of a male breadwinner in their household and used a husbands or son's proof of earning to obtain this visa.

Norma, a 35 year old domestic worker, also expressed concern over the documentation that she needed for the interview. Although she had sufficient money in the bank, her husband was out of work at the time that she applied for her visa, and so she did not have the required employment papers for her interview: "I just went to the bank and got a statement and then went to the pulga [flea market] and paid for some documents that stated that I was a vendor there; this is how many people get their visas, and with this I became eligible." Most domestic workers in this sample did not obtain their visa using false documents, but instead applied for the visa along with other family members in order to qualify. Women believed that if they applied as a family group, specifically with other women, their chances for approval would be higher.[10]

For many applicants, whether or not they were granted a visa was arbitrary and seemingly dependent upon the interviewing consulate officer's mood. Paulina had been working as a cross-border domestic for seven years when it was time for her to renew her visa to the newly-instated laser visa. She described her experience at the consulate:

> I didn't have any kind of documents. I was working on the others side [Laredo]. Who will give me proof of work? Who is going to give me proof of pay? No one can give me anything! But God helped me that day, and there we went without one paper. Now they are asking for papers from the bank, insurance, proof of employment, and expect you to have worked for a while at a job... The four of us went together, my mother, my son, my daughter and me. They took the paper that they had us fill out and that was it. He said, come here for a photo and they took

---

[10] Visas are given independently, but families have option of applying as a group and interviewing together with the consulate officer. Children under fifteen must apply with a parent and this visa expires on their 15th birthday (U.S. Department of State 2002).

the picture; and I asked, "All of us?" and he said yes. It was such good luck, and it doesn't expire until 2012, so I still have some time to go.

Although she communicated her visa renewal experience as a result of both chance and providence, Paulina had two major factors in her favor: she had been living in the Mexico border area her entire life and had been a border-crosser since she was a young girl. Her long stay in Laredo and her history as border crosser demonstrates to officers that she has not used her crossing privileges to enter the United States as a long-term immigrant. Newer residents to Nuevo Laredo do not have these advantages and, therefore, are often rejected when applying for this border-crossing visa; but because these women were assertive in their pursuit for labor in the U.S., they too found a way past these barriers.

Because providing stable employment is one of the requirements for this visa, many women, especially those who were younger and were new to Nuevo Laredo, applied for a crossing card while employed at local maquiladoras. Among the domestic workers in this sample, 35 percent of women received their border-crossing visas while employed at a factory. Bianca Ramon, a 23 year old live-in cross-border domestic, worked for seven years in a textile factory in Nuevo Laredo before she was driven to quit her job. Management at the factory had assigned her to supervise her peers, who were spiteful of her promotion and created an unbearable working environment for her. When she asked for a transfer to a different post, she was refused and found no other option but to quit her factory job. Since she had obtained a crossing visa during her time of employment, she turned to working full-time as a care taker for an elderly woman in Laredo, Texas. When I asked her if she had plans of returning to factory work, she stated:

> Yes, yes I do, because I will need to process my visa. You see, my visa will expire in the year 2010 and in order to renew it, I need to have proof of work that shows that I have insurance. I like factory work and I would also like my own business one day or something, but right now it doesn't pay too much. I will need to go back and work there for a year so I can renew my visa to work on this side [Laredo]. Here, the pay is much better and I have more money to buy things.

For Bianca, factory work serves as an avenue for future employment in the United States. She earns more than double her salary as a house cleaner compared to her previous job in the factory and is economically driven to continue working in Laredo.

Rebecca also gained legal entry as a border-crosser through her employment in a factory. After moving from a town in the interior of Mexico to Nuevo Laredo, several acquaintances advised her to find a job in a factory so that she could later process her visa and work in Laredo if necessary. She worked at an automobile factory for eight years, earning $70 a week while her husband worked on-and-off as a day laborer. After her divorce, she could no longer afford to make her house payments and support her mother and daughter on the wages she earned at the factory, "I couldn't make ends meet and so I had no other choice but to go to the other side [Laredo] to work." Mexican women have been relying on factory work as a means to gain entry into the U.S. (Quintanilla and Copeland 1996) even before the enacted changes in the border-crossing visas in 2001. These younger workers, especially those from the interior, utilize their status as formal workers in factories to upgrade their pay by becoming cross-border workers.

Employment in a factory, however, does not guarantee the easy acquisition of a border-crossing visa. Araceli Reyes, a 38 year old immigrant woman living in Laredo, had trouble qualifying for this visa when she was living in Nuevo Laredo. She was originally from San Luis Potosi, and had heard from relatives in Nuevo Laredo about the possibility of becoming a cross-border worker. She was reluctant to leave the ranchito, where she was living with parents, since her father was sick. But, her family needed the income and so she relocated to the Nuevo Laredo to live with an aunt. She said:

> I started working at the factory because I wanted to come to the United States with papers [legally]. Once I had been working for a year, I applied for the visa; I thought that I was going to get one, but they said that I didn't earn enough. When I started, I was earning 40 pesos [around $3.90 a day] and as months went by, they raised my pay to the minimum wage, and then I was earning 180 pesos [$17.50 a day]; and that is when they told me that I still didn't earn enough and to come back in one year. But I told them that I had all my papers and everything and they said that they didn't feel assured that I wouldn't be crossing to work. I kept trying but I didn't get it and I gave up after three years.

Eventually Araceli did become eligible for the visa and worked as a cross-border domestic worker for a few years. When she had to renew her visa, instead of spending the money on applications fees (which can cost over $100) that could lead to a rejection, she decided to let her visa expire and immigrate with her husband and children to Laredo to continue working in domestic service, yet this time without any documents.

Becoming a border crosser is not as simple as applying for a visa. Cross-border workers learn how to maneuver in this system and are assertive and persistent in their pursuit to become legal border-crossers. As the migration literature has demonstrated before, it is not the very poor who have means to immigrate into the United States. In the case of cross-border domestic workers, financial stability is important in determining who is eligible for this visa. Older workers who have become homeowners and have an established financial history in Nuevo Laredo have an advantage over newer migrants coming from the interior of Mexico. Those women who do not have the means to prove economic and employment stability empower themselves by working in local factories so as to later move on to the better-paying occupation of cross-border domestic work. Maquiladoras serve as an important means for the entry of young women into the United States and in the continuation of new cohorts of cross-border workers.

Migration and Empowerment

In recent literature on migrant women, the theme of women's emancipation has emerged as an important topic in understanding their gendered experiences in the United

States. Several studies have found that migration was an empowering experience for women in that it led to gains in personal autonomy and independence (Grasmuck and Pessar 1991; Guendelman and Perez-Itriaga 1987; Hondagneu-Sotelo 1994; Pedraza 1991). Women's increased participation in paid labor, their larger contribution to household finances, and as a result their increased decision-making in the household provide them with more leverage within the home than they had in their country of origin (Pessar 2003). This approach has been criticized for not taking into account the inequalities that are reinforced and maintained in the home, and the limitations that women experience upon migration (Parrado and Flippen 2005). These findings do not apply to the cross-border women in this study since they do not reside in the United States, but they do pose an interesting question: Are cross-border domestic workers disadvantaged in their personal relationships in the home by staying in Mexico? While many studies on women migrants survey both women and men in an attempt to understand the details of the home life and relationships among immigrant couples, this was not the primary focus on my study. But I did glean some insight into the issue from the conversations I had with cross-border domestic workers. The topics of empowerment and emancipation emerged in interesting ways, for instance, by women choosing not to immigrate and to stay in Mexico instead.

Popular ideas on Mexican immigration hold that most Mexicans would immigrate into the United States if they had the opportunity. Yet cross-border domestic workers defy this belief because, although they do have the opportunity to safely enter American border cities using their crossing visas, they choose to reside in Mexico rather than in the U.S. The majority of the cross-border workers in this study are intimately familiar with the opportunities that are available to them in the U.S., such as free public education and social benefits for the poor yet, despite this, they preferred their life in Mexico. For most women, living in Mexico provides them a sense of community that they believe is not available to them in the United States. For instance, Clementina Valdez, who once worked as a live-in nanny in Laredo, commented on life on the 'other side.'

> One does not have the same freedoms [in Laredo] as they do here [Nuevo Laredo]. Yes, there are many comforts and things that are nice, like air conditioning and all that, but here I just feel freer, as if I can do what I want. I can just go out on the street here and I will see so many people. Over there, only at the H.E.B. [local grocery chain] or Wal-mart are there people around; maybe even downtown, but that's it. I like life here. Even without all the comforts, life is better for me here.

Rosie Sanchez shared similar feelings about living away from Mexico. She had the opportunity to leave Nuevo Laredo when her husband was working in Laredo without documents as a truck washer a few years ago:

> R: My husband wanted us to join him on that side [Laredo], but I don't like the ambiente [ambiance] over there, and when he realized that we were not going follow him he came back.
> C: Why don't you like it?

R: Well, here people leave their houses. Like right now, look at the street: even though it's dark outside, you can see people passing by. You see people walking and you say, "Good Evening," "Good Afternoon," or "Good Morning." And you can go to a store and it will be open, even at this time. Around here, there are stores nearby, and over there everything is really far away. You have to go in a car everywhere and you don't see people on the streets. People just go from home to work and from work to home. And if you are at home, no one leaves the house because they are all watching television. I do like working there, but I wouldn't like to live there.

In these narratives, both Clementina and Rosie speak of the loss of mobility and a sense of community that living in the United States brings. Many cross-border domestic workers did not know how to drive and for those who did, their vehicles were not always reliable. These women walk to nearby stores for supplies and depend on the Nuevo Laredo bus system to take them across town and to the international bridge so they can travel to their employer's homes. In addition, these "freedoms" cross-border workers describe also allude to the reality that they are living outside their employers' homes, unlike immigrant domestic workers who often work as live-in maids. Unlike most other Mexican women considering immigration, cross-border domestic workers are intimately familiar with the lifestyle of the U.S., where neighborhoods are often zoned and a car is necessary in most cities in order to travel around town. In other Mexican migrant streams, elaborate tales about the opportunities in the United States and the comforts available in this country are passed through migrant networks, enticing newer groups of emigrants to cross the border (Hondagneu-Sotelo 1994). Against this backdrop, cross-border workers establish their own ideas and perceptions about life in the United States through their frequent entry into Laredo; they weigh its advantages and disadvantages, and use their own experiences of living and visiting the U.S. to make decisions about the nature of their migration, thus allowing for a new perspective on women's decision making.

As mentioned earlier, women who emigrate from Mexico to the United States have long been depicted as passive actors in the migratory process. Like their immigrant counterparts, the increased earnings women bring to the family allow them a certain amount of leverage in their households. Cross-border workers had an additional advantage in that, by "migrating" to Laredo, they earned more than their husbands who worked in Nuevo Laredo, making them the primary wage earners in their homes. Whether this has an effect on their gendered relationships in the home is unclear, but it does have an impact on their pursuit for labor. From my conversations with these women, I found that cross-border domestic workers are assertive and persistent in their pursuit to become legal border crossers. The majority of these women applied for their crossing visas independently from their husbands, often with the support of other female family members, and utilized all possible avenues in order to qualify for this crossing privilege. Since their earning potential was greater than their husbands', their pursuit for labor was both necessary and accepted by their partners, although perhaps begrudgingly by some. For instance, Monica Delgado

began working in Laredo as a housecleaner when she and
her husband purchased a home in Nuevo Laredo. She said:

> He has never believed that women should work. He
> thinks like they did in the past and sometimes he
> gets upset and will say, "It's because I feel bad; you
> earn more than me. I'm the husband!" And I tell
> him that he makes the house payment and pays for
> some bills. I tell him, "Your income just doesn't go
> far enough" and he gets upset. He doesn't really like
> that I work, but it's a necessity for us right now. If it
> was up to him I would not be working at all.

For many women, their husbands were accepting of their
labor in Laredo and welcomed the additional income. The
opportunity to legally and temporarily enter the United
States has enabled Mexican female border residents to
become active agents in their decision to cross the border to
pursue higher-waged employment outside of their home
country.

Although these women are advantaged by working for
comparatively higher wages in the U.S. while living in their
country origin, their temporary migration also comes with
disadvantages. Most cross-border domestic workers
expressed concern regarding the growing violence in
Nuevo Laredo. Since 2005, a major drug war has erupted in
this city, which once considered one of the more
peaceful border destinations in Mexico. Each day, these
women must travel through the Nuevo Laredo downtown
area where acts of violence frequently occur. Most women
were more concerned over the safety of their children, who
stay at home while they are working in Laredo. For
instance, in Carmen's neighborhood there was drug-related

shooting a few blocks from where she lived. Since she works four days a week in Laredo, she was worried about leaving her children alone at home.

> Before, when there wasn't so much violence, I could get home late and I wouldn't feel afraid. But now I'm scared. I'm also afraid for my children. They stay inside the house [while I am at work] and I tell them not to leave, to not answer the door to anyone; if someone knocks, they pretend that no one is home.

The freedom of mobility and sense of community that cross-border workers valued as Nuevo Laredo residents were restricted by the ongoing violence in their city. The few women who stated that they would prefer to live in the United States referenced the ongoing drug war as the primary reason.

Conclusion

As I noted at the start of this chapter, in the last thirty years, Mexican women have been entering the U.S. in unprecedented numbers and can no longer be ignored by social scientists and policy makers. By examining the motivations for Mexican women's migration into the U.S., as it has been understood in the migration scholarship, I attempt to understand and highlight the differences between those women who immigrate and those who commute across borders. The multiple factors that influence cross-border workers are very similar to other migrants in that they include poverty in Mexico, the demand for employment in the U.S., social networks, and personal experiences.   But they also differ in that cross-border domestic workers enter the U.S. primarily for employment, while long-term immigrants migrate to seek out family unification and later, to find work.

The means by which women become eligible for Border Crossing Visas, which allow them to temporarily enter the U.S., are crucial to understanding age and financial stability as influencing who can become eligible for these crossing privileges. Older women had an advantage in that they typically had obtained this visa before the requirements became more stringent in 2001. Women's strong desire to become cross-border workers was apparent in my conversations with them about their experiences in obtaining this visa. They were assertive and creative in their pursuit for international crossing privileges, thus challenge the depiction of Mexican women as passive followers of men in migration. Most importantly, this study reveals that the growth of export manufacturing in Mexico, as result of the Border Industrialization Project and NAFTA serve as a avenue for women to seek and obtain employment in the United States. Domestic work, which typically carries a negative stigma, is sought out and preferred over factory work due to the higher wages in the United States and the more flexible schedule it provides for women with families.

Finally, I discussed the topic of women's empowerment upon migration, which has also been a subject of debate in recent literature. The dual locations of cross-border workers who are embedded both in Mexico and the U.S. provides an interesting vantage point in this debate, which leads me to ask: Are women empowered by staying in Mexico? In the case of cross-border workers, who are employed in the U.S. and are the primary wage-earners in their families, their movement gives them the best of both worlds: life in their country of origin and increased earnings in dollars across the border. I find that their mobility and embeddedness in community and social life in Mexico, as well as their higher wages, serve as sources of empowerment. These issues were not the primary focus of my study. Nonetheless, they suggest that the question of women's empowerment in their homes subsequent to employment needs further specification in the literature on migration. A comparative analysis of cross-border workers with immigrant women could illuminate some of the contextual factors that either inhibit or enable women's empowerment and agency.

CHAPTER 4

Cross-Border Migration

Introduction

Gabriela Cantu lived in a two bedroom house with her husband and her two sons, who both worked at a local factory in Nuevo Laredo. A few weeks before our conversation, she underwent a hysterectomy and was taking time off to recover before returning to work as a full-time nanny in Laredo. She was a good friend of my research assistant, who seemed to have prepped her about the interview before we had arrived. As soon as I introduced myself, she asked us to sit down and offered us some lemonade. I then took out my tape recorder, and she said to me, "Yes, you probably will want to record what I'm about to tell you." She then began narrating a story about her experience working for an immigration officer in Laredo.

> I once worked for a couple [in Laredo] for only three days. I only lasted three days because my employer worked for Immigration. The Señora told me that if her husband ever came home with someone I had to hide…She would tell me, "If my husband comes home with anyone I want you to hide anywhere you can." I didn't like this because I didn't want to be thinking of hiding all the time.

Later that day the [house] alarm began sounding. They forgot to turn off the alarm; and so el Señor had to go home to turn it off, but he had forgotten that I was at his house that day... He got there with three friends from Immigration and they entered the house with him. I saw them and so I hid...I hid in the bedroom. He then started showing his friends his house. They were in the living room and then I heard them coming into the bedroom. Ahh! I heard them coming my way and I thought to myself, "Where do go?" I thought for a second that I would hide in the bathroom, but then I realized that the closet seemed like a better idea. I entered the closet and closed the door. As soon as I did they were all in the bedroom, and he was telling his friends, "Come over here...I'll show you this" and who knows what he was showing them— something that helps with seeing at night, and then he said, "I want to show you what I just bought" and he opened the closet door! As soon as he did, he saw me, and then he said, "Oh I forgot where I left it! We need to leave right now." Finally they left! ... I only worked there for three days because I don't like having to hide.

In my conversations with cross-border domestic workers, I found that like Gabriela Cantu, several women were employed by border officials or had been in the past and many other workers stated that they had friends who were working for immigration officials. The hiring of undocumented women from Mexico by border officials, whose job is to secure the border and apprehend illegal immigrants, reveals the complexities of this "border zone" in relation to the three major groups who inhabit this space: the border enforcement officials who knowingly participate or turn a blind eye to this unauthorized labor, employers who demand and expect cheap and undocumented help in their homes, and cross-border workers who must come into contact with both of these groups in their pursuit for employment.

The complex relationships between border officials, employers, and cross-border domestic workers as it plays out in the border city can be analyzed by examining the multiple spaces of the borderlands. Studies on the borderlands in the social sciences focus on the economic, political, and national divides which migrants transcend through their sustained and regular social contact across these divides (Levitt 2003; Portes, Guranizo, and Landolt 1999). Visible boundaries that separate borders are understood as "an appearance of separation between spaces where in fact what exists is an ambiguous continuity" (Lefebvre 1991: 87), an ambiguity that is dramatically instanced in the example provided by Gabriela. The border city that cross-border domestic workers enter is comprised of multiple spaces, which these women occupy on their journey to and from work. Space is defined as a "practiced place" (de Certeau 1984: 117) where they "interpenetrate one another and/or superimpose themselves upon one another" (Lefebvre 1991: 86). The practices of work and consumption construct different spaces within this border city. Understanding space as a practiced space allows me to examine how cross-border workers inhabit the spaces of the shopping area downtown, where they become consumers, the bus stops, where they are exposed as undocumented workers, and the space of employers' homes where they practice undocumented labor, yet feel protected from discovery. Analyzing these places as lived spaces also enables me to examine how officials differentially inhabit the multiple borderlands in this study. I am therefore able to unpack their interactions with domestics at the bridge, where they are employed to evaluate crossers upon entry, and compare these relationships that they have with daily crossers in their own residences and neighborhoods, where they are consumers of this undocumented labor. Officials' knowledge of and participation in the domestic employment of cross-border workers, as government employees and as private consumers, produces a more complex and nuanced attitude towards Mexican domestic workers than is evidenced in national policy discourse. Finally, by analyzing the practice of space, I can also understand employers' different attitudes towards migrants in their places of work outside their homes on the one hand, and in their homes where they are consumers of undocumented migrants' labor on the other hand. This chapter focuses on the shifting identities and subjectivities that are produced through the overlapping spatialized practices of work and consumption by all three groups who inhabit the borderlands.

As a means to understand the spaces that migrants traverse and transcend, scholars have developed the concept of "transnational social spaces," which are described as "pluri-local" and take into consideration the social spaces that span across geographic regions (Pries 1999: 6). In this chapter, I begin by discussing the actual process of entry for this population of women and how this determines who can enter the U.S. temporarily. I then analyze the cross-border movement of domestic workers in this "border zone" and the facilitation of this movement by employers and border officials. I examine the spaces that migrant women inhabit during their short stay in Laredo, and the different meanings they impart in shaping the identities of workers as they traverse through this border city. In addition, I also examine the social meanings of these spaces by analyzing employers and border officials, whose identities as producers/workers and consumers shift once they employ cross-border labor. Finally, I examine the means by which Mexican cross-border workers and employers locate employment in this border city and how these networks of knowledge are communicated in this "border zone."

Cross-Border Domestics as Consumers

When I met Maribel Delgado, she had just returned from work and was sitting outside her house, watching her children ride their bicycles up and down her driveway, relaxing for the first time that day. As we sat outside her house, busses in this late evening zoomed by filled with passengers. She pointed at one of the busses and explained to me that everyday she rides one from her home in Nuevo Laredo, Mexico to her workplace across the border in Laredo, Texas. In order to reach her employer's house every morning, she wakes up at 5:00 A.M. to cook breakfast, dress her children for school, and prepare lunch for her family. She then walks her three youngest children to school, accompanies her eldest daughter to her factory job, and then takes a bus to downtown Nuevo Laredo, where she walks to and across the international bridge. During our conversation she described her commute to Laredo at length. She said:

In total, it takes me about an hour to an hour and a half to get to work because sometimes the bridge is full. Here on this side of the border [Nuevo Laredo], there have been times when the lines are an hour or longer, but this doesn't happen every day. The other day, the line to cross immigration was half way down the bridge! By the time I got there [immigration] it was already nine o'clock. I got there and crossed and then they [Immigration Officials] checked what we were bringing, asked where we were going, and this and that. I didn't leave there 'till nine thirty, which meant that I had to wait for the ten o'clock bus. By the time I was at work, it was already ten forty-five or something like that. From the bus stop I have to walk. There are many ladies who walk twenty blocks! I only walk around five.

At four-thirty in the afternoon, Maribel leaves work and walks to the nearest bus stop, where she takes the same route back to Nuevo Laredo. By the time she reaches her house, it is close to seven o'clock in the evening and she has a few hours to tend to her family and rest before she does it again the next day.

For cross-border workers employed in domestic service in Laredo, their commute begins with a bus ride from their homes in Nuevo Laredo to the International Bridge #1, locally referred to as the "old bridge." This bridge connects the downtowns of Nuevo Laredo and Laredo and is the only bridge among the four that allows pedestrian traffic. Most women traveled from their homes to the bridge by relying on public transportation in Nuevo Laredo. Most neighborhoods are well-connected to the bus system. A few women who lived in the less-developed outskirts of the city relied on their husbands or a friend to drive them to the bridge. Travel time by bus to the bridge depended on the location of their homes in relation to the downtown. The average travel time to the bridge by bus was between half an hour to forty-five minutes. For those women who lived in the poorer neighborhoods in the outskirts of the city, travel time to the bridge was often more than an hour.

The vast majority of cross-border domestic workers enter Laredo on foot. Since traveling by automobile into Laredo is both time-consuming and expensive. While many women had access to a car, most did not know how to drive or did not own cars that were registered to enter Laredo.[11] Also, the fee to cross the bridge is significantly higher for vehicles ($2.00) than for pedestrians ($.35). Once they reach the bridge, their travel time varies depending on the length of the queue for inspection.

The cross-border movement of laborers who commute into a neighboring country to work for the day has been documented as occurring between other international borders across the world (Bouwens 2004; Schack 2000). Until recently however, very few studies have examined or even mentioned the phenomena of cross-border commuting from Mexico into the United States (Herzog 1990; Staudt 1998; Pisani and Yoskowitz 2001, 2002). The United States-Mexico border is unique in that although they share a 2,000 mile boundary, the economic disparities between these two countries are extreme, thus stimulating the cross-

---

[11] In order to drive into the United States, Mexican cars need to be registered, which can cost hundreds to thousands of dollars, depending on the vehicle.

border movement of workers. The frequent and recurrent movement of working-class Mexican woman across this international divide occurs in most border cities within the United States.

At this port of entry, over four million pedestrians and six million personal vehicles enter each year (United States Department of Transportation 2007). Cross-border workers are among a large population of Mexican border residents who enter Laredo temporarily using United States government-issued Border Crossing Cards (BCC), also referred to as "laser visas." The laser visa, which replaced the previous visa in 2001, is considered more secure than other crossing visas used in the past since it is a biometric card that includes fingerprints, a photo, and can be scanned upon entry. With this visa, Mexican residents are permitted to enter the U.S. within 25 miles[12] and up to 30 days for the purposes of visiting and shopping, but not to work (United States Department of State 2002). In order to take advantage of the laboring opportunities across national borders, these women use their crossing privileges to labor in domestic service in United States border cities. Their crossing, while not as physically dangerous as those women who enter the U.S. without documents, does carry with it a certain amount of risk. Before entering the United States, an immigration officer asks each crosser for documents that prove their eligibility. Cross-border domestic workers and other Mexican residents entering with the crossing visa present their Border Crossing Card to the officer. At this point, the officer studies the visa and chooses to scan it through the computer in front of him/her

---

[12] The exception is in the state of Arizona where Mexican residents with border crossing visas can travel up to seventy-five miles.

or immediately return the card to the border crosser. In my experiences crossing into the United States, rarely were border crossing cards scanned at the entry. Cross-border workers confirmed my observation. In my conversation with Alicia Navarro, a cross-border worker employed as a nanny, she disclosed her experiences when crossing through inspection at the bridge. "They hardly ever scan my visa. They just ask where I'm going and I tell them that I'm crossing to shop."

On each occasion that they travel to work, cross-border workers meet face-to-face with agents from three different branches of the United States Homeland Security (INS, Customs, and the Border Patrol). Since these women are legal crossers, meeting with these agents is simply part of their daily routine. Most women rarely experienced problems when entering Laredo. Rosie Sanchez, who had been working in Laredo for five years, crossed the border four days a week with relative ease, "It's very rare that they ask questions. Even now that I'm pregnant, they haven't been asking anything. And there are so many people who think that we just cross to have our babies." If suspected of entering the U.S. for labor, border agents can confiscate their border crossing cards and suspend the crosser from applying for this privilege in the future.

Thousands of Mexican residents enter Laredo for the purpose of shopping on a daily basis. The local Wal-Mart stores in Laredo boast the highest gross sales in all the United States (Gibbs 2000). The economy of the Laredo downtown relies significantly on the cross-border shopper from Mexico who is an important source of revenue for the Laredo economy. The Laredo Development Foundation, which is dedicated to strengthening the city's economy, estimated that cross-border shoppers contributed roughly 50 percent of sales in this city (Hall 2006). A study on 300 businesses located in the downtown of Laredo found that more than 60 percent of the sales were from cross-border shoppers (Owen 2002).

Upon entering Laredo as pedestrians, the first space border crossers encounter is the Laredo downtown. This downtown area, which was described by a local merchant as the "biggest flea market in the world," is filled with a variety of stores that cater to the Mexican shopper. During business hours, shoppers from Mexico dominate this area, making it a comfortable space for the cross-border worker to inhabit. Since Mexican women's entry into the country is tied to their activities as consumers, they can freely and legally occupy these spaces. This is an important shopping area for cross-border domestics who spent most of their wages on groceries and other goods in these stores. Juanita Gonzales said it best when she stated, "the dollars we earn in Laredo stay in Laredo." Workers preferred buying groceries and clothing in Laredo since they found that these items are cheaper and of a better quality than those that are available in Nuevo Laredo. Many women considered their privilege to shop as important as their entry for labor.

The volume of crossers that enter Laredo everyday place increased pressure on border agents to inspect entrants in a quick and efficient manner. The city as well as local retailers are concerned that increasing the wait times at the bridges will decrease the number of shoppers entering Laredo, which would have a dramatic impact on the local economy. As one representative from the trucking industry stated, "Every time we chisel away at the folks coming across from Mexico, we chisel away at our sales tax revenue" (Richards 2008). The current goal of tightening border-crossing from Mexico is met with pressure from the local community to allow the free flow of these consumers. Although cross-border domestics complained that their wait time to enter Laredo has increased dramatically since 9/11, they continue to enter by adopting the role of a consumer, which facilitates the entry across the border.

For the majority of women in this study, shopping was the primary reason given to border officers when they were questioned. Lupe Martinez, who worked as a caretaker for an elderly couple on weekends, found shopping as the best excuse to give officers. She stated:

> They ask, "Where are you going?" I say I'm going to the H.E.B.; that is where everyone says they are going and it's the truth because there are many people who don't go to Laredo to work, but they really are crossing to go to the H.E.B. For me, the truth is that I am going to go shop at the H.E.B.; that is, once I get off of work (laughs).[13]

So as not make border officers suspicious of their reason for entry, cross-border domestics prepared for the inspection and their encounter with border officials. Since the most common pretext for entering Laredo is shopping, women make a point to carry money in their purses in order to prove to officers that they are indeed entering for this reason. Carolina Alvarez, who had been working in Laredo

---

[13] H.E.B. is the major grocery store chain in Texas. In downtown Laredo, a H.E.B. store is located a few blocks from the international bridge, making it easily accessible to pedestrian crossers from Mexico.

for several months, was informed by other women workers on the precautions she must take when crossing the border to work: "I always take money with me, at least forty or fifty dollars because that's about how much people spend on that side [Laredo]. And if they ask where I'm going or what I'm going to buy, I tell them I'm buying shoes for my daughter or something like that." Daniela Cruz, who had once been taken to secondary inspection for questioning, learned to carry with her no less than a hundred dollars in her purse to prove that her intention was to shop.

> You need something more in order to defend yourself. Sometimes I will put some clothes on layaway, because you know that the stores on that side [Laredo] do that, and if I'm questioned, I will show the officer the receipt and say 'I have this on layaway and I'm going to put a payment on it.'

Some women are also cautious about the time of day they cross the bridge. Crossing too early might trigger the suspicion of officers, so many women wait to cross until the late morning, once most of the shops in downtown Laredo are open. Alicia Navarro, who works five days a week as a nanny and housecleaner, is cautious about the time of day she crosses into Laredo, "I cross late because when you cross early is when they ask a lot of questions. I know a lady who crossed in the morning and had her card taken away because they didn't believe she was going to shop." Most employers are aware of the risks these women encounter and therefore expect their employees to arrive at work after 9:30 A.M. Although the majority of women in this study stated that they were rarely questioned by border officials when entering the U.S., almost every woman had an anecdote of someone they knew who had lost their crossing privileges at the bridge.

Since immigration officials often search bags and purses, cross-border domestics are also careful about what they carry with them on their way to work. Lilia Garza, who crosses at least twice a week, was taken by surprise when an officer asked her to open her purse: "It was about a month ago and they checked everything in my bag. What worried me was that I had phone numbers in there, but the good thing is that the man didn't see them; if he had he would have torn my card." Carrying local phone numbers and addresses raises the suspicion of immigration authorities, therefore women are careful of the contents they carry in their bags and purses.

Employers are equally concerned about the mobility of their employees and often go to great lengths to facilitate the successful border crossing of a worker they have come to trust and rely upon. Terri Garza often has discussions with her housekeeper on the potential problems that could arise during her daily commute from Nuevo Laredo. She narrated a story of her employee's encounter at the bridge.

> T: One time she had trouble crossing. They were questioning what they were coming for. If you said, "I'm going to H.E.B.," which is what everyone answers, they wanted to see money. They wanted to see cash, exactly what you're going to shop with.
> C: And did she have money?
> T: Yes, she always has money. I mean, in fact, I give her money to carry so that she would always have money to show them.

Sara Riojas is particularly attached to the woman whom she hires as a housekeeper in her home. Her employee, Guadalupe, has been working for Sara's family for over 35 years. Sara is concerned about Guadalupe's border-crossing, especially since regulations at the border have been progressively tightening. Sara and her employee have discussed different options that could possibly legalize Guadalupe's cross-border labor. She half-jokingly said, "I thought about adopting her, but my husband just had an attack. That's the perfect solution, but he didn't like it." Amanda Molina, who has been employing the same nanny for her children for eight years, has a vested interest in keeping her domestic working in Laredo. Amanda had contacted a lawyer for advice on legalizing her nanny. Her lawyer informed her that without a direct family member sponsor, obtaining legal residence would be close to impossible. Employers depend on the labor of these Mexican women and are concerned about losing their employees.

Mexican women cross-border workers have an advantage over men who also seek to cross and work in that they can rely on the gendered excuse of entering to shop. Although male cross-border workers were not included in this study, many crossers commented on their observation of the treatment of men at the crossing point. Daniela Cruz, an employer, observed that men were treated differently than women:

> There are a lot of gardeners who also cross, but they are more likely to be taken inside for questioning than we are. When men are crossing with visas, right away they are asked: "Where are you going? Where do you work in Mexico?" Women can

defend themselves by saying they are crossing to shop, but for men it's harder, especially when they want to cross during work hours.

Although cross-border domestic workers enter the United States with the pretense of shopping, this movement of workers is controlled by the state. In their analysis of transnational migration, Sarah Mahler and Patricia Pessar (2001) call attention to the "gendered geographies of power," which take into account the multiple positions of power across varied terrains. They argue that gender and the state often determine who can move and who can stay. This concept is useful in understanding border officials turning a blind eye to the cross-border movement of women workers. In the experiences of cross-border domestic workers at the immigration checkpoint, border officials determine who can enter the United States border temporarily. Officials accept the gendered expectation that women are shoppers and play a key role in determining who can enter border cities temporarily for labor— in this case even labor that is undocumented.

As illustrated in the anecdote at the beginning of this chapter, the cross-border labor of Mexican women in Laredo is no secret to the immigration authorities. Several workers indicated that immigration inspectors know that they are crossing to work, but are not interested in stopping them. As Maribel Peña stated, "The migra doesn't want to send us back. Sometimes for fifteen days straight you will get the same officer when crossing. They don't switch officers each day so many of them recognize us." Clementina Perez, who worked in the past as a nanny for a Border Patrol agent, often saw her ex-employer when she was crossing through immigration at the bridge, "I say hello to him and I make a point to wave so that other officers see that I know someone who works there (laughs), in case they decide to question me. And he comes out and chats with me about how I'm doing and asks about my baby." Hiring a woman from Mexico to do the domestic chores in the home is way of life for border residents; therefore border security officers who live in this community are often tempted by this cheap and convenient labor.

Daniela Cruz, who works on the weekend as a caretaker for an elderly couple, was bragging about her connections through her employer and how that protected her from punitive reprisals if her work in Laredo was exposed.

> Everyone knows that we cross [to work]. Even they themselves [immigration officers] at the bridge joke with us and say, "Wal-mart or H.E.B.? You never say anything else." They themselves say that; and like the couple I take care of on the weekends, their son works for immigration and he said, "If you have any problems or anything, just call me," and their daughter in-law also works for immigration. She is actually one of the heads of all of the immigration officers. One time they had hired another woman to work here with me— it wasn't too long ago. Anyways, the woman, well since my sister is in charge here, she had decided to fire her for whatever reason. Well, when she [the new worker] found out [that she was fired] she said that she was going to report us [to immigration officials]…Well, my sister went ahead and called the daughter in-law who is the head of immigration. She told her what

happened and she [the daughter in-law] said, "Give me your information. If they take your visa away, I will just pick them [the visas] up and return them to you."

Border officials are an important group in the facilitation of the border-crossing movement of Mexican women workers. As one officer stated when asked about the large numbers of women who cross into Laredo to work as domestics: "Sometimes we'll have a complaint and we'll follow it up with an investigation, but it's low priority with us because it takes so much time" (Amir 1993).

In the past, the priority of border enforcement officials was to detect drug smuggling and illegal immigration. A border official in the Texas border city of Brownsville stated that after September 11th, "Our primary mission became to deter the entry of terrorists and weapons of mass destruction" (Brezosky, 2006). Domestic workers felt this change with the implementation of the new laser visas, which have more stringent requirements than the border-crossing visas in the past. Immediately following 9/11, border officials in Laredo began closely scrutinizing all persons who crossed the border, resulting in longer lines to cross into Laredo. The local newspaper, The Laredo Morning Times, followed the story of women crossers who had their visas confiscated by officials for not convincing them of their true intentions for crossing the border. One woman who stated she was crossing to shop at the H.E.B. had her crossing card taken away and was sent back to Nuevo Laredo (Ramirez 2001a). When questioned about this incident, one border official stated that it is out of place to deny entry to people who declare that they are entering to shop, but he stated that, "It's possible that [crossers] were vacillating when they answered [the inspector's questions]" which lead to their crossing privileges being revoked (Ramirez 2001b). These incidents occurred immediately after 9/11, but since then, all the cross-border domestics in this study stated having relatively few problems entering the United States.

Cross-border domestics' roles as consumers enable them to "pass" as legal visitors to the American side of the border. This facade is at least partially true, as almost all crossers also shopped in the stores that were located in the downtown shopping area near the border. Yet it is also stretching the truth, because they also engage in practices of work in residential neighborhoods as undocumented workers. It is ironic that their ability to engage in both legal consumption and illegal work is predicated on border officials' knowledge of both practices, since they are well aware that women cross for employment at specific times of the day and recognized their pattern of repeated crossings. It is precisely this insider knowledge of the social space of the border city that reassures them that allowing these women to enter, despite their illegal work, does not make them likely undocumented settled migrants. The gendered expectation of shopping that these women workers fulfill during border crossings illustrates the function of the "gendered geographies of power" (Mahler & Pessar 2001). In the next section, I examine the different spaces women inhabit on their journeys to and from work and their transitions from consumers to producers/workers.

Cross-Border Domestics as Producers and Workers

With the growing contention concerning the issue of illegal immigration in the United States, undocumented Mexican women and men constantly risk the discovery of their unauthorized status in this country. The few immigrant domestic workers I spoke with who were living in Laredo communicated their uneasiness about living as unauthorized residents in the United States and the daily risks they must contend with to work in Laredo. For instance, Anna Rojas, who had been living in Laredo for over 13 years, described her hesitation in driving her elderly employer on errands to the doctor and to the grocery store. While driving she makes sure not to commit any traffic violations in fear that the police could report her to border authorities. Ironically, the cross-border workers in this study have an advantage over immigrant women because they enter the United States legally and can legally move around in the space of the border city. Their legal status in the U.S. is complicated by their undocumented employment in domestic service. Cecilia Menjivar (2006) questions the dichotomous status of "legal" and "illegal" by developing the term "liminal legality" to describe the uncertain status of El Salvadorian political refugees awaiting legal documentation. This liminal status is relevant to understanding the experiences of Mexican domestics in the U.S. Unlike the El Salvadorian example, however, the legal status of cross-border workers is not in a state of transition or pending official change; instead, their legal status as "visitors" fluctuates depending on the particular spaces they inhabit, and the activities that they engage in within American border cities. The twenty-five mile radius that border-crossing visas allow these women to temporarily occupy is comprised of a combination of safe and risky spaces. The term 'liminal legality' does not apply to Mexican immigrant women since their status as both undocumented workers and residents does not fluctuate.

On their journey to their workplace from the downtown of Laredo, the majority of cross-border workers travel by bus to neighborhoods across the city. The main terminal of the local bus system in Laredo, El Metro, is located in the downtown, only a few blocks from the international bridge and has routes that shuttle these women to neighborhoods across the city. Domestic workers in Laredo are also an important source of revenue for the local bus system.[14] On any given weekday morning, domestic workers form long lines at the bus terminal waiting for their ride to work. In the afternoons, they congregate at bus stops in neighborhoods across the city. At bus stops, housecleaners and nannies become visible to the public. In Laredo, typically only poorer residents and pedestrians from Nuevo Laredo ride the local busses. Like most cities across the United States, most residents in Laredo drive from place to place, and only a small segment of the population battles the hot climate to sit and wait for public transportation. Once cross-border domestic workers board a bus and leave the downtown area; they also leave behind their identity as consumers and as a result of the spaces they inhabit, they become undocumented workers.

In neighborhoods across the city, cross-border workers walking to and from bus stops are often the only people on foot, especially in the more affluent neighborhoods in North Laredo. On Mondays, Wednesdays, and Fridays,

---

[14] Scholars have found similar patterns in other border cities. For example, in the border city of El Paso, the local busses cater to the large population of domestic workers who rely on public transportation (Ruiz 1987).

Monica Delgado walks several blocks in her employer's suburban neighborhood before reaching work.

> I feel as if any turn I make I might bump into la migra and they are going to arrest me...Downtown I feel very safe, but in the neighborhoods, once I get off the bus there are only houses around and if they stop me, how can I tell them that I'm here for shopping where there isn't even one store around!

Rosie Sanchez, who also walks a few blocks before reaching work, is similarly cautious on her way to her employer's house.

> Sometimes la migra drives by and I just say to myself, "if they stop and ask me what I'm doing here, what will I say?" The only thing that has come to my mind is to say that I came looking for a garage sale, but you know at the bus stops, there are so many of us [cross-border domestics]; a lot of people! I don't know if their hearts soften when they see us, but they have never stopped and asked questions, at least not when I was there.

Although domestic workers were cautious and often worried about occupying neighborhoods, in all the accounts and stories I heard from domestic workers about border officials confiscating a worker's border crossing card, all of those visas were confiscated at the bridge and not in residential neighborhoods.

Maribel Peña also expressed vulnerability when she walks the five blocks from the bus stop to her employer's home six days a week. She narrated an incident when she almost came face-to-face with the Border Patrol.

> In the corner of my eye, I saw that they [Border Patrol] were coming. I immediately thought that if I didn't get into the house soon they were going to question me, so I walked really fast. I got inside the house and asked la Señora to look out and see if they were coming, and she said they didn't return. She told me just to stay inside and if they came to the door she would tell them that I'm a friend of hers who comes to help her out. That's what we have planned.

The space inside employer's homes is where cross-border domestic workers expressed feeling safe and less vulnerable from being discovered by border authorities, even though, ironically, it is in employers' homes where these women violate the terms of their temporary entry by laboring for pay. But since border authorities do not typically go from door-to-door to catch these women in the act of cleaning, employers' homes serve as a sanctuary from the risks of their journey. A local news article reporting the Border Patrol's problems with apprehending Mexican maids stated:

> Catching maids working illegally is made even tougher because Border Patrol agents cannot enter houses without a search warrant, and no magistrate will grant a warrant without strong evidence that the family employs an undocumented maid. The evidence is lacking in most cases (Amir 1993).

Within employers' homes there are further distinctions between safe and risky spaces. As a means of protecting themselves and their workers, many employers discourage their employees from stepping outside when working. In many homes, part of the duties of housecleaners is to sweep outside driveways and porches. Domestic workers often expressed their uneasiness with this chore. Monica Delgado worked as a housecleaner in a home in an affluent neighborhood in North Laredo and part of her chores was to sweep the driveway. She said:

> I'm not too afraid when I'm walking [in neighborhoods] or when I'm on the bus. What I fear is that they will see me with a broom in my hand; that is what I'm most afraid of. On other occasions I can say that I'm going to visit my sister, but I don't have any defense if I'm sweeping.

On outside porches and driveways, neighborhood roads, and bus stops, the undocumented labor of domestic workers is most clearly revealed. While moving between these spaces along the border, their status as undocumented working-class Mexican women is exposed, adding to their vulnerability as workers. Riding a bus, walking along neighborhood roads, and sweeping outside are signals to border authorities that these women are poor and from Mexico. As I have stated before, very few women with legal documents work in domestic labor in Laredo. Therefore by occupying residential neighborhoods, especially affluent neighborhoods, cross-border workers can no longer play the role of a consumer thus exposing their undocumented status.

When they occupy these public spaces, Mexican domestic workers are visible to border agents as well as local residents. In our conversation, Yvette Guzman, an employer of cross-border domestic workers, was describing to me how almost everyone she knows hires someone from Mexico to clean their homes and how this goes on under the "watchful" eyes of border control officials. To explain the large population of domestic workers in Laredo, she said:

> You do see a lot of people [domestic workers], like in the mornings. On Saturday morning when you go and have breakfast or when you are driving to do your errands, you see the bus and everybody getting off the bus. They are maids and you can tell because they come at certain hours, usually in the morning and at three o'clock the bus stop is always full of people. [But] You never see the border patrol going around and asking questions.

Jessica Cardenas also observed the domestic workers who would walk to and from work in her neighborhood. She stated:

> When you pass by, you think they look like a maid…You know right away— you say, you know she must be a maid; I mean, she looks like a maid. You know they're always carrying their little bags around, when they go to work at a house they even stop and they… like the other day one of those ladies outside, you could tell that she was a maid, just [by] the way she dresses, the way she has her

little bags they carry... that's the way the border patrol spots them, I'm sure.

At bus stops and while walking in neighborhoods, cross-border domestics' inexpensive clothes and accessories only emphasize their undocumented status in these border spaces. In her analysis on the "placelessness" of Filipina domestic workers in Rome, Rhacel Parreñas (2008) found that women search for a space where they feel they can belong. Filipina domestic workers in her study were legally employed in domestic service and would live in Rome for years before returning home. In the case of cross-border domestic workers, who work without documents and return to their home country every evening, what is sought instead is a space in which they can be invisible.

In neighborhoods across the city, women's bodies as workers are more visible because the meanings of their bodies in space changes, from being read as consumers in the downtown and to being seen as workers in residential areas. However, employers and officers also make a similar shift in their embodied practices. In these residential areas, employers (specifically those who work outside the home), and officers (specifically those who hire undocumented household labor) make the transition from being productive laborers to consumers. Hence time and space carry social meanings that affect immigrant women as well as the other social actors— employers and border officials—that they encounter in these social spaces. It is this differential in the embodied practices of domestics, employers, and officials in these spaces, where they assume opposite roles as consumers and producers. These practices thus enable a symbiotic relationship between these three groups where the structure of the cross border migrant status is created and defined.

As stated earlier, social spaces must be understood in relation to time (Massey 1994). For cross-border domestic workers, their mobility through the downtown, neighborhoods, and bus stops are intimately connected to their temporality in these border cities. Since they return to their homes in Mexico in the evenings or weekends, employers and other community members have a different attitude about their presence compared to the unauthorized long-term immigrant population in Laredo. Employers and community leaders were concerned about the growing population of unauthorized immigrants who reside in Laredo. A representative for a social service organization in Laredo reported that the immigrant community placed a financial strain on the city and on the services of organizations— services that should benefit the city's needy legal citizens. Employers in Laredo were also concerned with undocumented immigrants living in Laredo and many were opposed to the "government handouts" that this population received. Jessica Cardenas, who had employed cross-border domestic workers for over twenty years, stated:

> I'm alright when it comes to the ones that cross and go back, like the maids. I think that's fine. I'm alright with that. But the ones that come illegally across are the ones that swim the river or they pay somebody to cross them; I'm not alright with that at all...I disagree with them crossing one hundred percent. Like I tell you, if they come over like the ones that I have working for me, they have their

card, they might not have it for working, but they have it, they come and work... but they go back! They're not going to suck the government because they don't [stay]. They go back and they live over there, and do not come over here so the government can take care of them.

Elaine Lopez, a young employer who was working as a nurse, had hired a full-time live-in nanny for the last six years. During our conversation, she also complained about Mexican immigrants living in Laredo.

Oh, I don't think it's fair. I don't, I don't know, I just don't think it's fair. How do these people have jobs and they don't even know how to speak English, their kids get to go to good schools, how? By using fake addresses? I don't think its fair for people who have to pay taxes. You know some people let their housekeepers have their children in the schools and its not fair for the tax payers to have that seat taken up by somebody who does not even belong in the district and your child doesn't even get a seat because this lady is using somebody else's address to put their kid in, you know. I don't think its right.

Employers and other community members, who are opposed to the influx of Mexican immigrants in their community, welcome the unauthorized labor of these cross-border workers. Rosario Dominguez, an employer of a full-time nanny, said it best.

> The way I feel about Americans is that everybody
> wants cheap labor, but nobody wants to let the
> Mexicans come in, and not just that, that's hard
> cheap labor, you know... that's who takes care of
> my kids, that's who mows my grass, that's who
> built our houses, like all those construction crews
> out there... like those are all, you know... that's
> who labor for us here in the United States and
> people don't appreciate that and they don't see it.
> They say oh look, close the borders and let's not let
> them in... that means prices are going to go up for
> everybody.

Employers' attitudes towards Mexican immigrants are
determined by the differential meanings that 'Mexican'
bodies take on in space and time. They seem more
comfortable with undocumented women occupying the
intimate spaces of their homes because it is temporary,
rather than their settling in the wider community of Laredo
where this stay is indefinite. Here, time transforms the
meaning of temporality and permanency, valuing the
former over the latter in their assessment of and affect
toward migrants. This means that cross-border workers'
presence and labor are generally welcome so long as it
remains temporary.

A few employers were sympathetic towards immigrant
workers. Terri Garza, who employs an elderly housecleaner
who had been a cross-border worker in Laredo for many
years, called the social security administration to find out if
her employee was eligible for benefits.

> I would like to be able to [legalize cross-border
> domestic workers]. I mean, whether you make them

legal or give them a permit, even if you don't do that, let us at least pay social security on these people so that we can give them a future. As it stands now, she [cross-border domestic] is going to be dependent on her grandson to take care of her— and the son of course, you know, I don't think he would ever take care of her; that's just the way he is. But the grandson is the one who will look after her because she has always taken care of him, and he's always told her, 'You don't have to worry about the future.' But I know they worry about the future. When she gets sick she worries about the future and I worry about their future. I don't think it's fair.

Most employers did not share this attitude and preferred cross-border laborers over long-term immigrant entering Laredo. In the next section, I continue to analyze the transnational spaces of the border by describing the methods through which domestic workers and employers contact and locate one another for employment in these borderlands.

Cross-Border Networks

Although the cities of Laredo, Texas and Nuevo Laredo, Mexico lie adjacent to one another, the distance between them can seem vast for Mexican women searching for work on the other side of the river. To overcome this barrier to employment, cross-border domestics and employers create and foster international linkages across borders. The information transmissions between these women are patterned and communicated through a gendered nexus of social relations. These social networks facilitate their movement, their access to employment, and their interactions with employers, which can be imperative in finding additional work. Domestic workers and employers communicate with individuals who serve as their cross-border transnational agents, who connect potential workers with employers and vice-versa. Mexican immigrants utilize social networks to secure employment before they leave their place of origin and again once they have reached their place of destination to pursue additional work (Hondagneu-Sotelo 1994). Cross-border domestics differ from the immigrant population in their social networks in that they draw on the social resources in their places of origin and destination simultaneously. These workers develop, maintain, and utilize their social networks on both sides of the border. In these social relations the "border zone" is produced as a transnational social space that transcends the distinctions of place in either country.

Cleaning agencies, such as Molly Maid, which specialize in placing women into jobs as housecleaners, do not exist in Laredo. For women living on the Mexican side of the border who are interested in working in Laredo as a domestic worker, finding and securing employment can be challenging. These women have two options: they can draw on their social contacts with friends and family or they can answer newspaper and radio ads posted by employers. Most cross-border domestics secure their first employment through informal social ties with other cross-border domestic workers and continue to use these contacts when searching for additional employment for themselves, family members, and close friends. Similarly, employers also use these social networks to locate a housecleaner, nanny, or elderly care worker by asking for references from domestic workers of friends and family.

In the literature on Mexican migration, the significance of social networks for potential immigrants and immigrants at the destination community has been thoroughly researched. Studies have found that Mexican immigrants draw on social networks in deciding when and where to migrate (Massey and Espinosa 1997), in planning their journey across the border (Singer and Massey 1998), in finding and securing employment (Espinosa 1997), and in sending remittances back home (Durand et. al. 1996, Mooney 2003). Social networks are especially important when seeking employment opportunities in domestic service. Latina domestics draw on informal social ties in learning job skills, finding employment, and negotiating wages (Hondagneu-Sotelo 1994, Mattingly 1999). Social networks also serve as a barrier to employment in that the lack of reliable social ties can impede women from securing jobs (Hondagneu-Sotelo 1994). Proficiency in English, legal status, and access to transportation also have been found to hinder many Mexican women entering the occupation in the United States (Mattingly 1999).

In recent studies on domestic service, Latinas in this occupation have been found to benefit from networks/ties with male migrant workers who work in gardening or who have contacts with potential employers (Hondagneu-Sotelo 1994, Mattingly 1999, Kossoudji and Ranney 1984); but among the cross-border population, male social ties are not as important in finding jobs. Most domestics are the only members of their families who work in Laredo, and therefore depend on female friends and relatives when pursuing jobs as maids in Laredo. In order for a cross-border domestic to be well-connected in this labor market, it is necessary to have reliable cross-border contacts with both women who are employed as domestics and who employ domestic workers. Most of the cross-border domestic workers in this sample were the only ones in their families who worked in Laredo. Since their husbands were employed in Nuevo Laredo, cross-border workers had to rely on contacts with other women. Informal social contacts between women function in introducing women into paid labor, in placing women in employment, in assisting with finding additional jobs, and in serving as a cross-border community.

The women with the strongest cross-border contacts were domestics whose mothers also worked as cross-border workers. Many workers in the sample were daughters of cross-border domestics and each of them were introduced and found their first jobs in this occupation through their mothers. The mothers of these women either referred their daughters to their employer's friends and family or gave up their position at a particular house to their daughter. Rosie Sanchez found her first job through her mother, who worked as a cross-border domestic for over twenty years, "I had always seen my mother working and then we started having a hard time with money— we just didn't have enough. So my mother told me to take one of her days and to start off with cleaning and I began from there." Through her mother, Rosie gained immediate entry into a job in Laredo. Building on her mother's contacts, she found work for four days of the week, alternating with six different employers. Carolina Alvarez also found work through her mother who worked as a domestic in Laredo: "My mother had hurt her arm and so in order to stay in her employer's good graces she asked me to take over until she

recuperated, but I just ended up taking over her job."
Although they gave their daughters entry into the
occupation, most women do not wish their daughters to
follow in their footsteps. Esperanza Navarro, who worked
as a live-in cross-border worker for an elderly couple,
discouraged her daughter from entering the occupation: "I
sometimes bring her to work with me so she can see
exactly what I do and how hard I have to work to earn
money."

Close family members such as siblings are also
important to women looking for this type of work. Daniela
Cruz found several jobs through her eldest sister, who has
worked for more than fifteen years in Laredo, "My sister
would bathe and care for a lady who had cancer. They
needed another person so she brought me in to do the
cleaning of the house. I worked there for five years and was
recommended to her employer's sister and their friends.
This is how I started." Daniela did not need any previous
housecleaning experience to find a job. She had a strong
recommendation from her sister who was trusted by the
employer. Social networks with other cross-border workers
are important for entering the occupation, but a
combination of networks with cross-border workers and
employers are important for building a full work week, and
for securing subsequent jobs.

For those domestics who did not have family members
working in Laredo, establishing social contacts with other
workers was crucial in finding employment across the
river. In most cases, these recommendations were from
close friends and less likely from causal acquaintances.
Lupe Martinez was from the interior of Mexico and did not
have any relatives in Nuevo Laredo. She found all of her

jobs through contacts with friends, "Sometimes a friend will come over and she will tell me, 'You know what? La señora who I'm working with has a friend who needs help. Are you interested?' And that is how I have found jobs sometimes." These cross-border friendship/social networks are vital for those women, like Lupe, who do not have family in Nuevo Laredo or who have only lived in the city for a few years. These interpersonal networks, however, did not always provide successful parings with employers and workers, especially when the contacts were acquaintances and not close friends. Lucia Hernandez experienced this when a church friend recommended a job opening with an ex-employer. "She said she found me a job that was for three days [a week]. I was so happy and thankful to God because they were going to pay me very well— $40.00 [per day] and everything. But it wasn't what it seemed at all and I ended up not liking the job." This particular employer did not like the way Lucia cleaned and continually scolded her throughout the workday. Although social networks are important in finding work, often domestics pass on jobs they are unhappy with to casual friends or acquaintances, who are often desperate for employment and may not be fully informed of the work conditions and the employer's particularities.

In addition to providing information about and introductions to potential new employers, women workers also served as a source of encouragement for women to enter into cross-border labor in lieu of other work opportunities. Women who had not considered working outside of the home were drawn into the occupation by friends and family who had strong social networks in Laredo. Before she married, Monica Delgado worked five days a week at an automobile factory. After marriage, her husband did not allow her to work outside the home. When her family began experiencing economic problems, Monica began considering returning to work.

> I began working in Laredo through the insistence of my friends Jessica and Thelma. They would tell me, 'Don't be a fool! We can find you a house to work at. Go for it! You are only making your life harder because you want to. Our lives aren't that hard.' More than anyone, it was Jessica who said, 'Come and help me and I will find you some work,' and that is when she found me my first job.

Lupe Martinez, who worked on the weekends caring for an elderly man, also began working through the encouragement of friends: "I had never thought about working on the other side [Laredo]. It was my friends who asked if me if I wanted to work at a house that they knew of and so I started." Lupe had also not been employed since she was married and did not join the paid-labor force until her friends had convinced her of the benefits of working in Laredo. Friendship ties among workers also extended to other forms of domestic support to enable women's work across the border. Monica and her two friends lived in the same neighborhood and became acquainted through their husbands, who worked in the same factory. Monica and her friends supported each other by scheduling their work days so as to ensure that one of them is always available to provide childcare for all their children while the others were working. These gendered networks enable many women to enter the paid-labor force as cross-border workers as well as find entry into the domestic labor market in Laredo.

Employer networks can also cause problems for some women in this occupation. When a domestic worker is unhappy with how her employer treats her or wants her pay increased, usually the only leverage they have is quitting a particular job and finding another to replace it (Hondagneu-Sotelo 2001). But when a domestic worker in a closely-knit employer network leaves one employer, this can place her other jobs in that same network at risk, especially if she works for a network of family members. Anna works for one such employer family network. She first began as a housecleaner for an elderly woman, and was then referred to her employer's two daughters. Anna works six days a week with these three employers and cannot financially afford to lose any of these jobs; but for the last year, she has been very unhappy working for the elderly woman. She has confronted the woman's daughter and daughter in-law with some of her complaints, but they both have asked her not to quit. If she leaves this job, she risks upsetting her two other employers, who rely on her to care for their elderly mother. Domestic workers in these family networks are at a disadvantage in that, so as not to risk losing their employment in the entire network, many women feel obligated to put up with abuse or mistreatment by one of its members.

Employers also rely on cross-border social networks to find employees. When searching for domestic help for themselves or for friends and family, employers often ask domestics for family or friend referrals. Olivia Perales is one of these employers. When her mother had a stroke, she hired Lulu to clean her mother's house and prepare her meals; but as the years progressed and Olivia's mother needed constant care, she looked to Lulu for additional help. She hired Lulu's sister and niece to give her mother 24-hour care. When Olivia's daughter, Lisa, needed a nanny, she hired Lulu's sister in-law to help with the baby. Once an employer has found a domestic worker they consider trustworthy and skilled at the job, they turn to their domestic's family and close friends as a means to hire other women who might have similar qualities. Olivia's friends and family rely on her to connect them with potential workers from Nuevo Laredo who are from a trusted network. Mexican American employers depend on Mexican domestic workers to connect them with other Mexican women with similar ethics and work values, utilizing their employee's cross border contacts.

Conclusion

In this chapter, I analyzed the cross-border movement of workers, the meanings of this movement in the different spaces that they inhabit in the city, and the connections they must establish across the Texas-Mexico divide in order to work in domestic service. In my analysis, I found that contrary to the literature on Mexican women's migration, Mexican women are assertive in their quest to successfully enter the U.S. for labor and relied on a variety of techniques to lessen the risks of apprehension. Under the guise of entering Laredo as consumers, border authorities allow poor Mexican women to enter the space of this American border city, knowing that many of these crossers enter for labor.

Unlike many cities in the interior of the United States where domestic workers are "hidden in the shadows," in Laredo, cross-border workers are a visible population.

Although their visas allow them to move within a 25-mile radius of the American border city, in spaces where they are visible as workers, such as at bus stops and in residential neighborhoods, and where their legality is in question, they are at risk of apprehension. I rely on the concept of transnational social spaces to analyze the different spaces these women inhabit on their journey to and from work.

Domestic workers experience different spaces as safe or risky as they navigate the border city on their journey to and from work through the downtown of Laredo. Cross-border workers feel safe and confident when occupying this area of the city, where they can blend in as shoppers. But as they move away from the downtown and into residential neighborhoods, they are no longer able to pass as shoppers and are exposed by their class, race, and gender as undocumented workers. Ironically, when they are in their employers' houses, where they are clearly violating the terms of their visa by using their crossing privileges to work, cross-border women feel most safe as long as their labor is contained inside the home. Likewise, employers and border officials also transition from being productive workers in the city to consumers of illegal services when they employ cross-border workers in their homes. This interplay of different meanings of shared social spaces intersect for the three sets of actors, and illuminates how the border city welcomes the cheap labor of Mexican women, as long as their stay is temporary. The obvious and well-known practice of Mexican women entering border cities legally as visitors to labor as undocumented workers is enabled by the complex and multiple meanings of transnational social spaces in border cities.

Border-crossing does not just involve the movement of people, but also the movement of information. Cross-border workers and employers rely on social networks to locate one another; and these networks must also cross borders in order to be effective. Women who are related to or have close friends working as cross-border domestics are most likely to find similar employment in Laredo. Employers also rely on the cross-border networks of friends and family as well as their household workers to locate a "good" worker. Cross-border workers who are established in the occupation are at the center of this economy of domestic work. Finding a job or locating a household worker involves navigating across national divides and producing "border zones" as transnational social spaces where knowledge crosses these divides.

CHAPTER 5

Culture, Class and *Comida*

Introduction

In the previous chapter, I described the movement and routine of Mexican women as they cross back and forth from their homes in Mexico to their workplace in the United States. I described how, for temporary migrants, different spaces take on different meanings in the transnational spaces of the "border zone" they inhabit. In this chapter, I examine how despite these transnational spaces created by the practices of workers, employers, and officials at the level of micro-relations between worker and employer, other boundaries are created and produced. These borders and boundaries in the lives of domestic workers span beyond the political and geographic divides they cross daily and permeate into the identity construction of both workers and employers. Working on the premise that the relationship between domestics and employers is inherently unequal, I analyze the production of difference and how it is negotiated between Mexican domestics and Mexican American employers. I use the examples of food, mealtimes, and mothering that emerged from my conversations with domestic workers and employers to understand how social boundaries are created and reinforced in these work relationships between these co-ethnic women.

To map out what follows, this chapter is organized into two sections. In the first part, I set the context for analyzing employer/employee relationships by discussing the labor associated with domestic service on the border. I begin with a description of "border culture" as it relates to the practice of employing domestic help and the perceived need local residents express for this labor. I then explore the multiple jobs associated with domestic service in Laredo. In the second section I examine how domestic workers and employers negotiate and define difference as a marker of their relationships. I draw upon theories of symbolic boundaries to analyze the production of difference in the work relationships between these two groups of co-ethnic women. I find that employers delineate and maintain symbolic boundaries through their control of material resources in the home, as a means to mark and maintain hierarchies of gender, class, and nationality. Domestic workers, who recognize and resist these inequalities, use femininity as a site for differentiating between themselves and their employers. In other words, Mexican domestic workers and employers reinforce and/or contest their status hierarchies through food preparation, consumption, and ideals of womanhood. These boundaries that are produced are not rigid, but are constantly challenged by both groups of women.

Domestic Work at the Border

In a series of articles for an El Paso newspaper, journalists refer to the local dependence on Mexican maids as the city's "worst kept secret" (Quintanilla and Copland 1983). In Laredo, paid domestic labor is also an integral part of the daily of life of middle and upper-class residents. Employers in Laredo have relied on domestic help for generations. Many employers in this sample grew up with nannies and housekeepers in their homes to later become employers themselves. Scholars Seemin Qayum and Raka Ray (2003) capture the practice of paid domestic labor in their description of the "culture of domestic servitude" in Kolkata, India. They describe this term as "the 'structure of feeling' associated with the institution, produced by the confluence of historical material conditions and prevailing social organization" (527). Although paid domestic work in Laredo does not have centuries of tradition as in India, this culture of servitude they describe is relevant to the attitudes of employers towards domestic labor, where the dependence on workers is considered part of "border culture."

Most employers, especially those with small children, could not imagine life without domestic help. Amanda Moreno, a single mother of two pre-school children who worked as a teacher at a local high school, had employed the same nanny/housekeeper since the birth of her oldest child eight years ago, as the child was very attached to her employee. In response to the onslaught of negative national media attention on immigrant workers, Amanda contacted a lawyer about possibly legalizing her employee. She also considered buying a used car so that her employee could travel around the city without fear of apprehension. Amanda commented on her dependence on her long-time worker:

> I would die without her! And I mean really because
> I need her to be there to watch my children when

I'm at work...She is very important to me; if I
didn't have her, I wouldn't be able to come and
work because my children are still young, and I just
can't be without her. It will ruin, well not ruin, but it
will change my whole life if she is not there.

Even those employers who did not have children or whose
children were already grown expressed the importance of
household help in their daily lives. Trisha Zuniga remarked
on her daughter's hesitation to hire a domestic worker:

I would always tell her, 'You need to get a
housekeeper,' because she is single and had all this
pressure from work. 'You need a wife is what you
need!' She finally got a housekeeper and she said
"God, I can actually enjoy my life now!"

Many women remarked on their privilege of living on the
border where there is a constant supply of low waged
domestic help from the neighboring city of Nuevo Laredo.
Yvette Guzman, who has lived in Laredo for the last thirty
years said, "Here in Laredo I think all of us are spoiled. We
are very used to having help and are so lucky!" Lisa
Barrera, whose parents are native to Laredo and has lived
in the city most of her life, also commented on the opinion
of her friends who live outside the border region and
questioned her reliance on domestic help: "They don't
understand the part a maid plays. It's not that you don't do
anything in your own home; they just make life easier, and
if you can have them, why not?" In the next section I
discuss the labor involved in domestic service in Laredo
and how this border culture is reflected in the wide range of
jobs associated with this occupation.

In Laredo, being a "maid" involves an array of activities that span beyond the quintessential task of cleaning. The term "maid" is used across town by local residents to describe women working as housekeepers, housecleaners, nannies, ironing ladies, and caretakers for the elderly. Both cross-border domestics and immigrant women work in these jobs across the city. As noted in the previous chapter, the majority of cross-border domestics are employed as live-out workers, but many also live-in with employers during the week or on weekends. Since this labor is cheap and in abundance, employers can afford to pay workers to do an array of different household and caring tasks that are all classified as part of "maid's work." Anthropologist Maria de la Luz Ibarra (2000) finds that the result of the influx of immigrants along with the changing global economy has restructured the occupation to include employers from diverse economic backgrounds and has expanded the labor associated with this occupation to include work such as elderly care. This "new" domestic labor she describes applies to cities in the interior of the United States where large pools of low waged female immigrant labor is a relatively new phenomenon. In the next section, I briefly describe the jobs associated with domestic work in Laredo, in which paid household labor has historically been a part of the economic structure of the community. This section is organized by the different jobs associated with domestic work.

Housekeeping

Paid housekeeping is a common in Laredo. Women in this type of employment work four to seven days a week for one employer on a daily basis, typically with the weekends free. The work of housekeepers in Laredo differs from employer to employer. Maribel Peña, a cross-border domestic who worked six days a week as a housekeeper for a large family in Laredo, described her duties and routine on a typical workday.

> I get there in the morning and I make breakfast... And then, on the refrigerator I have a menu that I make myself; this week I will make chiles rellenos, enchiladas… I write this menu, and I show it to her [employer] and then I will make a list of what I need, and then she will write me a check to take to the store. Yes, I also go to the store. I go alone and she lends me her truck. I do everything! During the day I'm running around everywhere. And then, after I come back with the groceries, I take them down and put them away, then I need to mop, clean the living room, the kitchen, the dining room, the three bedrooms and the office. I also dust everything. From there I go running to clean the bathrooms. Thank God there are only two bathrooms! Then I hurry because it's almost time to make dinner. I cook and in the cooking is where most of my time goes.

Many domestics are employed in jobs where they are expected to do much more than just clean and tidy-up, they also do the work involved in running a household. This could involve cooking at least two meals a day, picking-up children after school, planning meals, shopping for groceries/supplies, helping children with homework and, in some cases, light gardening. In places in the interior of the country, jobs of this nature are usually common among live-in help, but in Laredo, many day-workers are also employed in housekeeping.

In most cases, housekeepers in this study began working for their employer a few days of the week as housecleaners and as time passed, employers decided that they preferred their employee come to work all week to help with the household chores. Other women began as nannies and then, as the children grew older, continued working as live-in housekeepers.[15] Elena Ruiz, a 60 year old cross-border domestic, has been working for the same employer for over twenty-five years where she has been responsible for all the cleaning, tidying, washing, and ironing for the family. When she began this job, her employer had a family of seven, but as the years passed and the children of this house grew-up and moved away, her work load diminished substantially. Although her employer lives alone and no longer needs full-time help, her employer continues to hire Elena for the entire week knowing that Elena needs the work. When her employer is out of town, Elena continues to report to work everyday to do basic cleaning, take care of pets, answer the phone, pick up the mail, and generally keep the house occupied. Her employer relies on her not just for the daily chores related to running a household, but also her constant and regular presence in the home for security while she is away.

Jobs as live-out housekeeping are coveted among cross-border domestic workers since this work is steady and involves only one employer. Live-out housekeepers are typically paid by the week with the average weekly wage

---

[15] In Laredo, most employers preferred live-in nannies, especially when they had young children.

being $150. In addition to their pay, some employers included daily bus fare and bridge tolls, but the majority did not.

Nanny work

Working as a nanny is one of the most demanding and strenuous jobs in domestic service in Laredo. Since nanny-work is mostly live-in, the women most likely to work as nannies are recent migrants in need of room and board and steady pay (Hondagneu-Sotelo 2001). Of the different jobs in domestic work, nannies are more vulnerable to exploitation than any other workers. Their work hours are long, usually beginning in the early morning and ending late at night once all the children have been bathed and put to bed. Most women in domestic service try to stay away from this occupation and prefer cleaning jobs or elderly care. Live-in nannies are paid by the week, not by the day or hour. They usually work almost twice as many hours as housecleaners and have the added responsibility of caring for young children.

Sociologist Pierrette Hondagneu-Sotelo (2001) characterized the work of childcare providers as "nanny/housekeepers," and rightly so. In Laredo, most nannies are responsible for caring and looking after young children as well as cooking, cleaning, tidying up, and ironing. Most of the employers of nannies in this sample were working mothers of diverse class backgrounds. Employers stressed that their main qualification when looking for a child care provider was someone who would give their children quality care and attention. Yet, as much as employers indicated that cleaning was secondary, it was expected as part of the duty of a nanny. Most domestics found a way to accomplish both tasks. Valeria Cantu, a 55 year old live-in caretaker of a newborn, whom I interviewed while she was on the job, commented on her employers work expectations, "I do a lot of work for $150 a week. I clean, like right now I'm doing the laundry, and I do this all while I'm carrying him just like this (she motions to the baby in her arms) because he doesn't like his crib." Valeria and other nannies must multi-task when caring for young children in order to finish all of the work that is expected. Those women who work as nannies for school-aged children are also expected to clean their employer's house and look after the children once they return from school and during the summertime.

Housecleaning

Domestic workers describe this type of work as limpieza, which literally translates to "cleaning." Women working as housecleaners are all day workers, entering their workplace in the morning and leaving that same evening. Most housecleaners work at a single employer's home one or two days a week, filling the rest of the week with other day jobs. The length of a work day varies according to the size of the house and the expectations of the individual employers. Also, the frequency of cleaning a house makes a significant difference in the amount of work that has to be done at that particular workplace.

The pay for housecleaning is typically higher than that of live-in nannies and housekeepers since housing and meals are often calculated as part of the live-in workers wage. The average wage of a housecleaner was $33 for a six hour day. Rosie Sanchez, who had been working as a domestic in Laredo for five years, had six different employers. She worked four days a week and cleaned a different house each day alternating with two employers on Tuesdays and cleaning another house once a month. Each of her employers paid differently, ranging from $27 to $50 per work day. Fifty dollars is very high compared to what most domestics earn in Laredo. Of all the women interviewed for this study, Rosie's daily wage at this job was the highest. When describing her work at one of her jobs she said, "It's hard because there are three and a half bathrooms, four bedrooms, and the kitchen and living room to clean. But I'm happy because I'm alone and don't have to rush. When I finish my work I can leave. No one tells me I have to arrive at a certain time or work till a certain hour. I get there, do what I have to do, finish and I go." In this house, Rosie hardly ever interacts with her employer and lets herself in and out of the house with a key that they leave for her outside in a designated place. Many women prefer working alone and at their own pace, away from the watchful eye of their employer.

Ironing

Ironing clothes is usually included as part of the daily work routine for most women working as housecleaners and housekeepers. Those families who have excessive amounts of ironing, or who cannot afford to hire a full-time domestic, hire women whose sole job is to iron. Unlike drycleaners and professional launderers, domestic workers are not paid by the amount and types of garments they press, but are paid by day or half-day. Domestic workers in this sample earned between $22 and $35 per day for ironing. Rosie Sanchez, who irons for her employer once a week said, "Each week that I iron there is about four feet of clothing I need to get through. The pile never gets smaller. I just hope it doesn't get any bigger." Domestics considered the job of standing in one place in front of a hot iron as placing an increased strain on the body; therefore most domestics in ironing only worked in ironing jobs once or twice a week and filled the rest of the week with housecleaning. Lisa Barrera, a busy mother of four and a teacher at a local elementary school, could not afford to hire a full-time housekeeper. She does her own house cleaning but hires someone else to come in every Saturday morning to iron her family's clothing for the week: "I really need the help with the ironing. My sister says to just take them [the clothes] out of the dryer and hang them but I can't stand that. Even if my son just wears t-shirts, he's at the stage where the t-shirts are stained and stuff, but they are perfectly ironed because I don't like for it not to look ironed." The abundance of low-waged labor in Laredo allows for women from a variety of economic backgrounds to hire outside help for this burdensome task.

Elderly Care

In Laredo, the occupation of domestic service goes beyond housekeeping and nanny work. Undocumented Mexican women cater to the increasing demand for inexpensive yet high quality elderly care (de la Luz Ibarra 2001). In homes across Laredo, cross-border workers and immigrant domestic workers fulfill this need by caring for the elderly in private homes. The type of care ranges from elderly women who just need company, locally referred to as damas de compania, to 24-hour elderly care in which women are hired to work in shifts to care for sick or elderly persons. These workers, who typically have no medical training, monitor blood pressure, administer oxygen, regulate medicine, and decide when it is necessary to call a doctor or an ambulance. In addition, these women are also responsible for the grunt work associated with elderly care such as changing bed pans, giving sponge baths, and dressing and feeding the elderly and sick.

As the life expectancy of individuals continues to rise, care for the elderly has become a critical issue for Mexican American families. In contrast to popular beliefs, the majority of Mexican American elderly typically do not live in extended family units (Torrez 1996). Elderly who qualify for government assistance are provided a visit from a caretaker once a day by the state, who assist in bathing, feeding, and other tasks that are a challenge to the elderly. Middle and upper class families living in border cities have the option to hire cross-border and immigrant workers to care for their aging parents. Employers whose elderly parents are well enough to be cared for at home hire domestics to work in their parents' homes as live-in caretakers. Other families bring their aging loved ones into their own homes where they also provide constant care with the help of domestics.

Sandra Guevara, who lives with her elderly mother, hired several Mexican women to assist her with the cleaning, bathing, feeding and all other responsibilities that are involved in caring for her 92 year old mother:

> Well, mother was able to move, actually walk on her own up to about, I would say six or seven years ago, she was able to walk with a walker, but in the last six or seven years, mother couldn't get up by herself so I needed to hire somebody not just to take care of the household, but to take care of mother. And since mother is heavy set in all, I needed two people to help her get up and so on. And since then,

right now I hired three people, but they are on a
rotation basis, but there are always two people here
at one time.

It is common in Laredo for employers to hire more than
one person to care for their aging parents. Most domestics
worked in shifts where two domestics were hired to live-in
for the week, each taking turns to attend to the person at
night, and the next shift would work on the weekends. Like
live-in nannies, in many households, elderly care workers
were also responsible for the housework. But, since in most
cases more than one domestic is hired to care for an elderly
person, housework is often divided among the workers. For
instance, Sandra, quoted above, rotates the duties of the
domestic so that while one is caring for her mother, another
is tending to the housework.

Hiring a woman from Mexico to care for the elderly is
not restricted to the employer's or elderly person's home.
Women are hired to care for individuals who are living in
nursing homes as well. Employers, who have little trust in
local managed care facilities, hire Mexican women to
monitor the treatment their parents receive and to give their
parents the necessary attention they need that the nursing
home might not be providing, and to act as spies on the
quality of care that is provided. Jimena Mendez hired four
women, whom she referred to as "sitters," to watch over
both her parents in a nursing home.

The beginning of the sitting was making sure that
they ate, how they ate, and if the staff of the nursing
home were bringing the medications on time.
Actually, they were my eyes and ears and were able

to tell me what kind of a day they were having. They would call me in case the medicine cart had not come by, if it was already 2-3 hours past the time, and would also let me know about their emotional health. My mother would cry a lot they would let me know "your mother's been crying a lot today." I could not be there all the time. I still had a household and a husband and my other activities, and so I could not be there every single minute with my parents, so she did that. At that time she [domestic worker] was in the nursing home, she didn't have to change pampers or spoon feed. But they recorded everything for me. What time they had eaten, how much they had eaten, would they have slept and how much they had slept.

Like most employers, Jimena trained each of the women herself on how to care of her parents. Since she did not have the time to care for her parents herself, she relied on Mexican domestics to monitor her parent's condition.

Caring for the elderly is a stressful job that involves many responsibilities. Many women in this line of work are worried about the day their "patients" become ill or even die under their care. Veronica Marroquin, who worked as a live-in caretaker for an elderly woman who was recovering from surgery, worried about the well-being of the woman in her care. She said:

After she has breakfast, I give her the medicines. I have to keep checking that she's not going to take them on her own because suddenly she will grab them and she want to take them herself. I have to be more watchful of her because she can get up on her own now. Before, I had to be behind her to lift her and now she does it all by herself and she gets up. I have to be aware of everything she does because suddenly she will say that this is not her house and she wants to leave, and I'm afraid that one day she will try to leave. [emphasis her own]

As a live-in cross-border domestic, Veronica worked five days a week caring for this elderly lady, and was responsible for her well-being while she was in her care. Working as a caretaker for the elderly is a job that often goes into the night, and in this way it is similar to the work of nannies. Domestics must wake up and escort the person they are caring for to the bathroom and attend to all their other needs. Esperanza Salazar, who worked with her sister caring for an elderly couple, complained that she was working too many hours for what they were paying her. "Forty for the day and night they pay us. This simply means that for the day they are paying us twenty-five dollars and at night fifteen. But we hardly sleep because the woman finishes praying at twelve-thirty and then I give her a pill so that she can sleep. And then she will tell me, "I wet myself, change me!" And so I will get up, change her and then a few minutes later she is calling for me again."

Like all other forms of domestic work on the border, most caretakers for the elderly are paid by day and not by hour. The average wage of a caretaker was $45 per day as a live-in worker. This wage is higher since employers see this as a "more advanced" form of domestic service. Jimena Mendez, who paid the caregivers of her elderly parents more than she paid her housekeeper, justified the differential wages through the education these women brought to the job, "See, housekeepers are not used the higher level of thinking of reading and writing and I can't just hire anyone to take care of my parents. They had to have standard skills in reading and writing in Spanish and basic math and computational skills." Despite this claim, there was little difference in the educational background of housekeepers and caretakers for the elderly in my sample.

Mexican Domestic Workers and Mexican American Employers

In Laredo, Americans citizens rarely ever work in domestic service. A small minority of Mexican women with green cards also works as maids, but these women typically do not have the English language skills to find employment in other lines of work. Domestic labor in this border city is a reflection of the social class divide between Mexican cross-border workers and Mexican American employers who share and interact in the intimate spaces of the home. This section explores the status hierarchies that are marked and legitimized in the work relationships between employers and domestics through the management of material resources at the workplace, specifically food and meals, and through the production of an idealized construction of womanhood in these relationships. Food is considered a culturally defined substance that is important for creating and maintaining social relationships, "both to solidify group members and to set them apart" (Mintz and Du Bois 2002, 109). In the private space of employers' homes, food represents a material resource that employers utilize as a means to produce and maintain difference from the Mexican women in their homes. Michéle Lamont's (1992) theory of symbolic boundaries is relevant in analyzing the production of difference between domestics and employers.

She defines symbolic boundaries as the "conceptual distinctions that we make to categorize objects, people, practices, and even time and space" (Lamont 1992, 9). Lamont argues that in addition to developing and maintaining social groups, boundaries "potentially produce inequality because they are an essential medium through which individuals acquire status, monopolize resources, ward off threats, or legitimate their social advantages" (12). Pei-Chia Lan (2006) identified two distinct types of boundaries in employers' homes: those that separate the private and public domain and those that distinguish class and nationality between employers and domestics.

I also rely on the construct of symbolic boundaries in exploring these relationships, but I differentiate between boundaries that are produced by middle and upper-class Mexican American employers from those produced by Mexican domestic workers. I found that employer boundaries are created through the control of material resources in employers' homes to mark differences in gender, class, and nationality. Domestics also produce symbolic boundaries, but since they do not have control over material resources, they use "traditional" ideals of womanhood as a means to differentiate themselves from their employers. Although most Mexican American employers in Laredo do not overtly or even intentionally set boundaries between themselves and their employees, these differences are often communicated during mealtimes and in insidious, implicit practices rather than through overt discourse.

Consumption of Food and Mealtimes

The management of food in the workplace reinforces the hierarchies of gender, class, and nationality in the relationships between Mexican domestic workers and middle and upper class Mexican American employers. Employers often exercise their authority in the home through rations, meticulous inventories, and/or the denial of food. Cecilia Vela, who had been working in Laredo since she was a teenager, gave an example of the control her ex-employer exerted over her consumption at the workplace:

> In the mornings she would leave an egg outside the refrigerator for me and had all the bread counted. Her refrigerator had a lock by the way. "I'm going to give you one to eat," she would tell me. And she would leave the egg and bread on the counter, and this is what I would eat in the mornings.

It is uncommon for homes in Laredo to have locks on refrigerators, as employers do not need locks to limit and restrict the food consumption by maids in their homes. Monica Delgado, who had been working for her employer for six months, had never had a meal in her employer's home or attempted to eat any food from the refrigerator during her seven hour work day: "She has never offered me food before and I just don't feel comfortable enough in that house to eat anything. I have this feeling as if I eat something she is going to notice. I'm not sure if the Señora checks or not to see if anything has been eaten, but I just feel as if I can't take any of it." Employers do not need to be physically present to limit the consumption of their employees. Most domestics felt as if the Señoras of the house kept a mental inventory of the food in the refrigerator and pantry.

For most cross-border workers, the restriction and regulation of food is a daily occurrence, which begins when they cross the international bridge from Mexico into the United States. Pork, poultry, and certain fruits and vegetables cannot be brought into the U.S. from Mexico. Even for those who choose to bring "approved" food items from their homes, carrying a packed lunch into Laredo can be risky. In a routine inspection, border agents search handbags and other articles for any indication that may reveal their actual intentions for crossing. Domestics consider carrying a packed lunch from home across the bridge a clear signal to border agents that they are entering Laredo to work and not shop. Typically, cross-border domestics have a long commute to work, often only having time in the mornings for a cup of coffee and a small breakfast before heading to the bus stop. By the time they arrive at work, they have traveled on at least two buses, waited in line for inspection at the bridge, and walked several blocks to reach their workplace. On their modest wages, purchasing food during their journey can be expensive, and since the vast majority of domestics typically rely on the local buses, traveling outside the residential neighborhoods to purchase a meal is impractical.

Since most cross-border domestics cannot bring their own lunch to work, whether or not they eat during the day is at the discretion of their employer. In the case of live-in workers, meals are typically included as part of the work agreement. But for day work, it is often unclear whether meals are to be included in these work arrangements. Most domestic workers believed that, for a full work day, their employers should provide at least one meal. Many employers are also in agreement and feel as if it is their obligation to feed day workers. Brenda Gomez, a thirty year old elementary school teacher, described her attentiveness to the needs of her cross-border domestic worker in regards to meals:

> I either make her a sandwich or I give her good leftovers from the day before. If I don't have time to fix something for her, my husband will buy her a sandwich. I want her to be happy. She works from eight to four, so she gets very hungry. She also wakes up at five in the morning and has to walk a mile to the bus and the buses by her house aren't that regular; so when she gets here she must be really hungry [emphasis her own].

Many employers provide both breakfast and lunch for their employees, but some believe that providing meals is not their responsibility or assume that their domestics will help themselves to the contents of their refrigerator. In Mexico, the most important meal of the day is in the mid-afternoon and the meals in the morning and the evening are typically less substantial (Long-Solis and Vargas 2005). Therefore, when an afternoon meal is over-looked or denied, domestics consider this behavior an egregious form of mistreatment.

The quality of the food that is allocated to domestics is also an area of contention for many workers. According to Pei-Chia Lan (2006), "status distinctions between employers and maids are displayed by hierarchical distribution of various kinds of food – expensive versus cheap, meat versus vegetable, subsistence meals versus snacks, and fresh food versus leftovers" (203). Often if a domestic is given a meal during her workday, she is given a portion of what the family is eating. But in many cases, inexpensive food is set aside for the worker, while employers eat fresh and name brand quality items. Women working as live-in help were most likely to experience this distinction in food provision. Esperanza Salazar, a 44-year-old live-in caretaker for an elderly woman, commented on the meals her employer would give her. She said,

> She [the employer, Eva] had food for months that was frozen or in the refrigerator …she would make this food for us to eat. And one day I became very sick from what I ate, and Señora Carmen [Eva's sister] told me not to eat what Eva would give us because Eva would sometimes give us food that was over three months old! She will never just give us fresh food.

Women in this occupation often complained that the food that was left for them was different and lower in quality than what the employer and her family would eat. Maribel Peña, who worked for a short period of time with another domestic in a large home reported:

> The young girl who was working with me saw me take a Coke Classic from the refrigerator, and I opened it and drank it. The young girl saw me and said, "No!" And I just looked at her and said, "What?" "Don't drink those Cokes because they are going to scold you," she said. "Why can't I drink these Cokes? Look I'm already drinking it," I told

her. "If the Señora finds out that you drank these, she's going to scold us." And I asked her, "What do you mean she's going to scold us? I like these Cokes. Do you want one?" And I opened it and gave it to her... The ones that were name brand were for them! For us, they gave us the cheap stuff, just like the milk. They gave us the cheaper milk, see?

In this example, Maribel describes the class boundaries that her employer sets to differentiate workers from family members in food allocation. These boundaries reflect the Señoras communication of class differences through the allocation of the "good" food for the family and the "cheap" food for the worker. But Maribel asserted herself by taking, and giving her co-worker, a "forbidden" soda. This example shows how, although employers have the material resources and power to delineate difference, domestics continually cross and contest these boundaries.

The difference between domestics and employers is most clearly communicated with the separation of domestics from employers during meals. In most cases, domestics eat in the kitchen or in a separate room in the house away from the family. Domestic workers often eat after their employers have finished their meals. Some workers withstand hunger for hours until they are given permission to eat lunch. Lilia Garcia, a 45 year old cross-border worker, expressed her frustrations over mealtimes in her experiences as a maid in Laredo:

I was working for a woman once who in the very first week told me, "You're not going to eat right now because my husband gets angry; you will eat later." And I told her, "Señora Carolina, you can give me my food anywhere, but please just give me food. I don't expect to sit down at the table with the rich people when I am poor! I don't need to sit at the table with you. Just have me sit anywhere; it doesn't matter." So I would just sit in the kitchen to eat, and sometimes I would have to endure my hunger for a long time before it was my turn to eat.

Lilia associated their social class differences between her and her employer as determining where and when she should sit and eat at her workplace. Juanita Gonzalez, a 62-year-old domestic worker, reflected on the last 40 years that she had worked as a housecleaner and the various ways in which her employers had made her feel subordinate to them.

I worked for a person who would ask you to step down to the patio while they were eating. Yes, to the patio! They would send me outside and would tell me, "sweep this over here while I eat." When they would finish eating, they would have me come back inside. And then they would say, "he didn't eat very much; eat what's left over" because there was no food left; they had already eaten everything. They would actually store what was leftover and would say, "Look, she didn't eat all her food, so you can go ahead and eat that; anyways it's clean." They would feed you from their leftovers [food that remained on plates]. There were several persons who were like that, but I was in need of the job so I wouldn't tell them "no."

Her employer's demand for privacy during mealtimes and her practice of allocating picked-over food from their plates sent Juanita a clear message about her inferior status.

Mary Romero (1988) found, in her study with Chicana domestic workers, that it is not uncommon for employers to sit and eat with domestics, but employers are the ones who most often either join the domestic for a meal or do the inviting. In Laredo, the practice of sitting separately from domestic help is common in homes across Laredo, and most employers do not consider this demeaning or insulting towards domestic workers. In a few cases workers and employers did sit together. In my conversation with Lisa Barrera, a 36-year-old teacher, she casually described the eating arrangements for her employee in a brief moment of our conversation. She said, "I do feed her breakfast, I prepare breakfast for everybody, and when we are done, I serve her. I tell her come and eat. And her breakfast is ready, and she will eat whatever we eat."

Most domestics do not expect to sit with their employers during a meal or even eat in the same room as their employers. In her study on Latina domestic workers in Los Angeles, Hondagneu-Sotelo stated, "Sitting down to share a meal symbolizes membership in a family, and Latina employees, for the most part, know they are not just like one of the family" (2001: 34). In my conversation with Rosie Sanchez, a 24-year-old cross-border domestic, she narrated an incident where she was taken by surprise at a mealtime. She stated,

> I had just met La Señora... I thought that since this is a new job that she would treat me differently, but no, she treated me really well. She even, notice this,

it was the middle of my workday, and she asked me if I wanted her to heat up some food for me, and I said, "Yes." And she heated up the food, and she called me when it was ready. I went to go eat, and she had even made food for herself, and she sat with me to eat! Can you believe that? These are things that many people don't do. Many, many people say, "Why am I going to sit over there with her?" and other stuff like that. But not her; she sat with me to eat.

The hierarchies of social class and gender in these relationships were not only communicated through the denial of food or segregation from the family, but were also communicated when employers went out of their way to treat an employee as if she was "one of the family." Since maids cannot refuse an invitation to eat with their employers; in effect such invitations are also experienced as an order. Maria Fernandez described just such a situation during mealtimes with her employer.

On Fridays, she always sends me to pick up lunches for everyone, hamburgers, fries, and everything. And I sit to eat with her at the table. "Come and sit down Mari," she tells me. "No, no, no. Don't go into the kitchen to eat. You're crazy; sit with us?" And I ask, "Señora, can't I just take it with me on my way out?" "You will sit down," she says. She has two older sons who are also eating at the table, and I just feel so uncomfortable. Every week it's the same, every week.

On other days of the week, at the insistence of her employer, Maria eats lunch with the Señora of the house. But on Fridays, the family eats together and Maria especially dreads these meals. For some domestics, sitting with their employers during meals directly violates the social class hierarchies of their relationship, which often causes both women discomfort. Employers who insist on shared meals challenge these barriers, yet they do this using the authority that their positions provide. Although these employers are making an effort to include their employees in their personal space during mealtimes, this is being executed through coercion. Maria does not have the authority to decline sharing a meal with her employer, leading to an uncomfortable environment where their status differences are reinforced.

In most cases where employers and employees sat together to share a meal, this meal involved only the employer and the domestic. When other family members were present, domestics typically ate separately. For instance, Olivia Perales, who hires two live-in cross-border domestic workers during the week, describes the eating arrangements in her home:

> They like to eat separately. Sometimes they eat before my husband and I get home. And sometimes when we come home late, they eat before us since they cook what I tell them to and they eat the same thing we eat. But in the mornings, since my husband goes to work early, I usually have breakfast with them. We talk and we read the newspaper together, and we talk about things that we need to do around the house.

Since her husband is absent for breakfast, Olivia uses this time to chat with her workers, but she also uses this time to give them instructions for that day. When domestic workers share a meal with women employers, these are often informal often taking place in the kitchen and involving a simple meal. When and employer's husband or older son is present, the dynamics of the meal change and mealtimes become family centered, which typically exclude domestic help.

Those domestics who expressed a favorable relationship with their employers had a sense of autonomy at their place of work. In our conversations, Daniela Cruz, who worked seven days a week with five different employers, considered her Tuesday employer her favorite. When I asked her to describe why she liked this particular job, she said,

> In this house, I treat it as if it were my own (laughs). When I get there and I get out of the bus, and La Señora is there waiting for me, and so when I get to the house, my plate is there served for me so I can eat breakfast. Sometimes there are revueltos with herbal tea. And I serve myself a glass of juice, a glass of milk, or whatever I want to drink and a plate of fruit every morning... They leave the house, and they think about what I'm going to eat. They go out to eat every day. But if they don't, she tells her husband to go buy me a hamburger with fries from McDonalds, or if they are going to eat out breakfast and have some breakfast tacos, she will say, "Olga, wait for me. We are going to bring

breakfast here." They are people who are so sweet that I can't say enough about them.

Letty Ochoa had a similar relationship with her employer. She began working with this particular family when her employer began receiving treatments for breast cancer and was not healthy enough to do the cooking and cleaning in her home. After her employer recovered, Letty continued working at this job. When asked about her relationship with her employer, she said,

> I get along really well with La Señora. We talk and sometimes we even eat together; these are on the days that she doesn't have work. She buys us food and we sit and eat, and then she makes coffee and she asks me, "Letty, do you want some coffee?" She makes me the coffee, and we sit and we drink coffee and just get along very well. [emphasis her own]

Letty describes the closeness she feels with her employer through her description of these periodic meals they share together. In both of these cases, Daniela and Letty felt comfortable with their employers and enjoyed their interactions during their workdays. Domestics who had autonomy in their food consumption and during mealtimes had a positive attitude about their work environments and in their relationship with their employers.

Ideal womanhood

Although Mexican cross-border domestic workers are marginalized by class and race, they also mark and maintain the difference between themselves and their employers. Unlike their employers who communicate their status difference through their control of the material resources in the home, domestics produce difference through their constructions of womanhood that are based on the ideals of the "authentic" Mexican woman. Traditional gender ideals regarding women in Mexico involve the space of the home, where women are responsible for all domestic-related tasks and family life. These ideals, which are based on a rural lifestyle (Mummert 1990), have been significantly transformed with urbanization and women's entrance into paid labor. Yet, despite these changes, employed women in urban settings continue to be primarily responsible for household labor (Fernandez-Kelly 1983).

Based on their observations in the homes of employers, domestic workers used these meanings of womanhood to distinguish themselves from their co-ethnic employers. In the examples below, food is once again used to express these differences:

Everything they buy is from a box and a can, and we don't buy like that. We actually cook our food. For example, they buy beans from a can and rice; well, all they do is put it in the microwave and it's done. And here [Mexico] we don't do that. Here we add the condiments; we add onion; we add the garlic, etc. And over there they don't. There they buy everything frozen, and all they do is thaw it, and it's already cooked. Yes, it's very different here.

Compared to her employers in Laredo, Rosie Sanchez views her own cooking as superior since she uses only fresh ingredients and does not feed her family frozen or processed food. By comparing their "homemade" style of cooking with that of their employers, domestic workers emphasized their adherence to their ideal notion of the Mexican woman who cooks and tends to her family.

Maribel Peña was especially critical of what she considered her Mexican American employers' lack of effort in the kitchen. She said,

> They like the American customs. They hide behind them because they are lazy. They hide behind the other culture, see, because you know that the American does not eat the way that we Mexicans do. For the Americans, it's very easy. The food is very easy to prepare. It's canned or things like hamburgers. Even the hamburgers now, they just put them in the microwave and they're ready. You just put the food in the microwave, and it's cooked. So, the lazy Mexican on that side [Laredo], well food is their life for them because that is what they don't cook. Because, notice, la Patrona, the one that I'm working for now, she says to me "Oh, Señora, I used to make food that was so good." She says, "I don't know what has happened to me now." She tells me that she used to make calabacitas rellenas de carne de puerco. That's work! She used to make golobanes. She used to make empanadas, and now? She just comes to see what is being made so she can take it and eat. Yes, they are lazy because they do know how to cook. [But] It's rare for a Mexican woman not to know how.

Maribel excuses non-Hispanic employers from this label of lazy since she considers using prepared food as part of the American culture, yet she condemns her Mexican American employers who rely on similar cooking methods. Mexican American women are expected to make an effort in their cooking since they are of Mexican descent. In both statements above, the ideals of femininity and Mexican authenticity together create superior values and practices of an "authentic" Mexican woman. Through these distinctions of gender and nation, they produce difference in relation to what it means to be a real Mexican woman. Cross-border domestic workers value their lifestyle and devalue that of the Señoras by producing an ideal woman, one that follows traditional Mexican values.

Employers were not silent when it came to the food domestics prepared. Many employers enjoyed their employees' cooking and specifically requested their employees to prepare certain dishes. Others were critical of the domestic workers' style of cooking. Jessica Cardenas, a 55 year-old homemaker and employer for over twenty-five years, preferred to cook her own meals: "I don't let the maids make dinner for me because they use a lot of spices, and they just use a lot of grease. Even if it's oil, I mean they use so much oil that I just can't stand it, so I'd rather do it myself."

Domestic workers also used styles of mothering to distinguish themselves from their employers. The act of mothering has a greater social significance than any other aspect of femininity to idealized constructions of womanhood. In Mexican culture the responsibility of motherhood lies with women. Motherhood is seen is seen as natural, universal, and unchanging (Glenn 1994).

"Motherwork" is understood as extending beyond the biological needs of children and families to also include identity, and group survival (Collins 1994). The literature on domestic service pays close attention to the actual practices of mothering that domestics are engaged in as part of the duties of the occupation (Hondagneu-Sotelo 2001, Wrigley 1995). Recently, research has focused on "transnational motherhood" in which migrant domestics who are living abroad, continue to manage and care for their families across time and space (Hondagneu-Sotelo-Avila 1997, Parreñas 2001).

Most domestic workers prided themselves on their knowledge of home-related tasks and considered it important to pass on these skills to their children. For the cross-border domestics in this study who most often see their children on a daily basis, their roles as mothers are central to their identities as women and as workers. Mothering was often used as a means to offset differences in class and nationality between themselves and their employers, who they identified as inattentive to their children. Juanita Gonzalez, who had worked as a housecleaner for the same employer for over twenty years, commented on the kind of education her employer gave her child:

> She might be very rich, but she didn't know how to educate her daughter...she sent her to school; she was taught there, but she didn't give her an education on taking care of a house and of values. And even though I was poor and everything, I taught them [her own children] how to work since they were twelve-years-old. They would go out and wash cars, polish shoes... and her daughter, she

doesn't take care of the house; she doesn't do anything. Nothing, and in that, I feel superior.

Juanita's six children only completed school until the sixth grade, yet she considers the education she gave her children in relation to caring for the home and learning the value of work as superior to her employer. Domestic workers value their practices of mothering over those of their employers, despite the latter's financial advantages.

In addition to seeing themselves as better mothers, many domestics who worked as housecleaners stated that they were also required to be attentive to the needs and circumstances related to their employers' children. Domestic workers were often aware of private details involving the lives of their employer's children. In many cases domestics felt obligated to inform employers of private details and activities involving employer's own children. For example, Juanita Gonzalez was first to suspect that her employer's teenage daughter was pregnant and communicated her suspicions to her employer:

> It turns out that Alejandra was four months pregnant, and she [Juanita's employer] said, "Well it's good that you're the one who noticed it." Of course I'm the one who is going to notice these things!" I told her, "I didn't have many daughters, but [with] the one I had, I was careful to pay attention to everything was going on."Domestics often described this sense of themselves as better mothers using examples from their experiences of working with families in Laredo.

Women working in domestic service also questioned their employers' priorities as mothers in comparison to their own lives. Mexican American employers who worked full-time were often seen as adhering to what they considered "American values" that place more importance on material possessions than on raising a family. Lucia Hernandez explained this when describing her experiences with employers in Laredo, Texas:

> They don't just want to have one car; they want two or three. They don't want the house they have anymore; they want a prettier one. And this is their logic, so the bills and the payments are higher, and so they have to work more hours. And in the time they actually have with their children, they think they can make up being gone with these things, but you can't because this is time that you will never get back!

The feminine values associated with mothering are connected with ideals of traditional Mexican culture that reflect the boundaries of nation that domestic workers create to define themselves as mothers and essentially as women.

Most domestic workers were not critical of their employer's choice to work outside the home; instead they questioned their employers' reasons for choosing to work. Most cross-border domestics in this study were the primary earners in their homes. In our conversations, the school tuition, grocery bills, and house payments that these women were struggling to pay were central to their discussions on motherhood. In her study on Mexican American and Mexicana working mothers, Denise Segura (1994) also found that Mexicana women considered economically providing for their families as an extension of motherhood, while Mexican American women internalized white middle-class views of paid employment as oppositional to motherhood. Domestics in this sample also associated their employment with motherly duties, yet saw themselves as superior to their employers whom they perceived as not working for their children but instead for material consumption.

Of course it is worth noting that the criterion by which domestics were judging their employers would also set them up as failed mothers. The production of symbolic boundaries of ideal womanhood are based on how Mexican domestics ideally would like to be as mothers and do not reflect the constraints they encounter as working women with families. For example, although domestics were critical of their employers' lack of time with their families, they too spent long hours at work. Cecilia commented on her employer's inattentiveness to the television programs that her children watched, disagreeing with the adult content they were often exposed to. "I always have my children here with me. I'm always watching them and everything, and I make sure to monitor what they watch on television." In reality, Cecilia worked six days a week in Laredo, Texas and usually did not return to her home in Nuevo Laredo until late in the evenings

Mexican American women also referenced domestic workers when reflecting on their own duties and responsibilities as mothers. Unlike domestic workers, employers rarely witness the home life of their employees, yet they associated mothering with the freedoms hiring a domestic provides. Employing a domestic worker is integral to practicing the type of mothering they viewed as important, which involves spending less time cooking and cleaning and more quality time with their families. Cleaning, cooking, and washing are activities that can be passed on to someone else, so that they can participate in "higher" forms of gendered activities. Rosario Dominguez, a 32-year-old lawyer and mother of two, hires a live-in domestic to care for her children and clean her house while she is working. "You know, I don't want to have to do my laundry, and I don't want to have to clean my house, not if I can pay someone. This time can instead be spent with my family!" Many employers in this sample grew up with maids in their homes and most have employed household help their entire adult lives. Hiring a domestic worker not only frees employers from gendered activities of the household, but also allows them to partake in other activities they consider more important than dealing with the "dirty work" of household chores.

Conclusion

In this chapter, I began by describing the array of jobs that are associated with domestic labor in this border city. The wide-spread practice of hiring domestic help among the middle and upper-class Laredo residents and the abundance of cheap household labor is evident the different types of jobs associated with line of employment. Hiring inexpensive household help in this border city is considered part of border culture and an advantage of living so close to Mexico. Domestic workers are eager to cross borders and participate in this labor that pays higher wages compared to their home country. Yet, at their workplace, they are once again confronted with borders in their relationships with Mexican American employers. Domestic workers challenge these boundaries and, in the process, create their own forms of difference.

In these "sister cities," employers living on the American side of the border create and maintain symbolic boundaries to distinguish themselves from the Mexican women they employ. These boundaries, which employers establish through their control over the material practice of food management, reinforce the power hierarchy of the relationship between domestics and Señoras. Who eats, what is eaten, and where and when domestics eat, communicates the inequalities of gender, class, and nationality in these class relationships. Boundary-making in these relationships contributes to the degraded status of the occupation of domestic workers which justifies low wages, heavy work loads, and inferior treatment for this group of working women. Examples of segregation during mealtimes, meticulous inventory of food, and allotment of inexpensive food for maids compared to the employer's eat, reveal ways in which social class inequalities between employers and employees at the workplace are communicated. In the literature on domestic service in United States, inequalities of social class between employers and their maids have been tied to race differences, since white employers are typically compared to employees who belong to other racial or ethnic minority groups (Hondagneu-Sotelo 2001; Romero 1992; Rollins 1988; Dill 1988). Since the women in my study are co-ethnic Mexicans, class hierarchies in employer-employee relationships can be analyzed independently from race. Yet, social class in these examples is complicated in that it is produced through gender and nationality. Cross-border domestic workers deployed the gendered distinctions between themselves and their employers through examples that represent ideal womanhood that is specific to their reference of the "authentic" Mexican woman. Therefore, although these co-ethnic women allow for social class to be teased out from race, gender and nationality continue to complicate the relations between these two groups of women.

Domestic workers recognize the hierarchies of gender, class, and nationality in their work relationships and confront these inequalities by also producing difference. Since they lack control over material resources at their workplace, they create distinctions to demarcate a superior sense of self by using the material practices of ideal womanhood. By critiquing their employers' food preparation and mothering practices, domestic workers create their own distinctions in relation to the "authentic" Mexican woman and, in so doing, produce identities that enable them to encounter the indignities of class that they face on such a routine and intimate basis. By producing these boundaries of femininity as it relates to Mexican authenticity, they are communicating the ideals they value. Although the Patronas are also acting in accord to their own ideals and values, cross-border domestic workers dismiss these as inferior to their own worldview.

CHAPTER 6
Migration Without Settlement

In light of the increased migration of women workers across the globe, this study addressed Mexican women's labor migration in a context in which there was no migratory settlement. In this study, I examined the following questions: What are the material and social conditions that influence some women to immigrate into and later settle in the U.S., and others to become long-term commuters? How are the meanings of social spaces—such as that of 'home,' the 'workspace,' and the spaces in-between—transformed by this frequent movement of workers? And how does this cross-border movement shape the meaning and structure of co-ethnic employee/employer relationships? In this chapter, I briefly review the major findings of my study. I then address the limitations of this study as well as topics for future research and the questions that have emerged from it, which I intend to pursue in my future research. Finally, I conclude by focusing on the future of this form of border-crossing in reference to the increased tightening of the U.S.-Mexico border and its implications on cross-border domestic workers and border communities.

Cross-border Domestic Workers at the U.S.-Mexico Border

The topic of women's migration is relatively new to migration studies. Up until the 1980s, women's migration was ignored and considered secondary to that of the male migrant (Pessar 1999; Pedraza 1991). Since then, as women's movements across the world have dramatically increased, so too has the scholarship on women's migration. Migration is inextricably linked to the experience of settlement, which is the dominant framework that has been used to understand women's migration experiences (Hondagneu-Sotelo 1994; Glenn 1986; Grasmuck & Pessar 1991). The temporary migration of women workers across national borders has largely been ignored. Most of the interdisciplinary literature of migration, especially that of Mexican migration, understands the movement of workers as either long-term or as cyclical. This study expands upon the migration literature by examining women's migration outside the framework of settlement by analyzing the frequent and recurrent movement of Mexican working-class women across national divides, who "migrate" for labor and yet who do not settle in the United States.

To understand this form of temporary migration by Mexican women who live in border cities, I began by reviewing the multiple factors that have contributed and continue to motivate the migration of Mexican women to the United States. Women's emigration from Mexico to the U.S. has been attributed to several major policies, including the Bracero Program, which initiated a pattern of male migration and, later, women's emigration (Hondagneu-Sotelo 1994) with the Immigration Reform and Control Act of 1986, which tightened the borders with Mexico, resulting in an onslaught of male-worker settlement and, ultimately, the migration of women for family unification (Durand et al. 1999; Cornelious 1992; Massey et al. 2002). The Peso devaluation of the 1980s contributed to dramatic wage decreases and the rise of women entering the workforce (Tiano 1994; Gonzalez de la Rocha 1993). Gender relations in the home also contributed to women-centered networks facilitating migration for Mexican women (Hondagneu-Sotelo 1994; Lindstrom 1991; Massey & Espinosa 1997).

This study challenges the general assumption that women's migration into the United States is passive and primarily undertaken for the purpose of family unity by analyzing a different form of migratory movement. Women's cross-border labor at the border provides a different perspective on women's decision making and motivations for migration that is not revealed in traditional migrant studies. Women in this study were assertive, persistent, and creative in their decisions to become wage-earners in their households and in their efforts to secure Border Crossing Cards, which allow them to practice this form of cross-border labor. I found that financial stability is a major indicator of who becomes a cross-border worker. Since the main objective of this visa is to allow Mexican residents to visit and shop in American border cities, border officials want to ensure that crossers enter for shopping purposes and not for labor or long-term settlement. The majority of cross-border workers were homeowners with extensive financial histories, who had resided in Nuevo Laredo for more than ten years. Women who were "older" (in their thirties) typically had these resources and therefore comprised the majority of my sample. Recent changes in the eligibility for Border Crossing Cards in 2001 have made obtaining this crossing privilege harder than it was in the past. I found that older women had an advantage since most had the previous version of the crossing visa and could prove to officers that they had both a financial history and a long history of border-crossing. Part of the requirements for obtaining this visa is proving employment. Since cross-border domestic workers could not take proof of their undocumented earnings in the United States to their consulate interviews, they often had to depend on a male relative to prove financial support. In reality, cross-border workers who worked full-time in Laredo were the primary earners in their households.

I found that younger women who did not qualify for the border crossing visa found an alternate means to obtain this crossing privilege. In order to become cross-border workers in Laredo, many women who could not prove their financial stability worked at a factory job in order to establish employment history. While working at a factory for a minimum of a year, Mexican women could prove evidence of their employment to border officials and become eligible for this crossing visa. A large proportion of women in this sample left factory work for cross-border domestic work, which pays almost three times their salaries at a factory.

Although the stringent regulations in obtaining a border crossing visa that were enacted in 2001 have made this form of migration more difficult for Mexican border residents, it has also enabled a particular group of women to thrive in this labor market. Older women, who are at a disadvantage as workers in Mexico, especially in factory work where younger workers are preferred, have an advantage over younger workers in qualifying for this border crossing visa because they can more easily provide proof of their financial stability. This requirement for a visa filters out many of the younger workers who compete with them for jobs in the labor markets in Laredo and Nuevo Laredo. Since these regulations limit the number of women who are eligible for this visa, they limit the pool of available workers competing for the same jobs.

Mexican cross-border domestic workers were also aided by their choice to live in Nuevo Laredo and commute to Laredo rather than become long-term migrants. In contrast to the popular belief that Mexican immigrants seek long-term settlement in the United States, I found that cross-border workers, who were intimately familiar with life on both sides of the border, preferred to reside in Mexico instead of the United States. These women expressed a sense of community that was not available in cities in the U.S., where people tend to keep to themselves and where neighborhoods are zoned. In addition, they expressed the "freedoms" they experienced by living in their own country and not having to worry about being undocumented compared to long-term immigrants.

Living in Nuevo Laredo enabled cross-border workers to earn a higher wage in domestic service in Laredo than they would if they were employed in Mexico in factory work or domestic service. With their earnings, these women workers invested a portion of their income in home equity and property in Mexico while spending on consumables such as food and clothes, in the United States. The narrative of domestic service as "dirty work" is thus complicated by this form of migration. For working class women in Mexico, domestic work in Laredo is a coveted occupation that is often preferred over factory work and other occupations available to them in Mexico. Cross-border workers empowered themselves by choosing to live on the Mexican side of the border and commute to their jobs in the United States.

For most women, the commute from their homes in Nuevo Laredo to Laredo is long and involves taking multiple busses and walking several blocks, often in the extreme heat of the Laredo climate. Their determination to cross the border for labor is apparent in their commute to Laredo. Since most women in this study were the primary earners in their homes, their successful passage through the U.S. border inspection each day was a primary concern in their commute. Equally important to their employment was their desire to shop in Laredo for groceries and household goods, which were at a considerable savings and of better quality than similar items in Mexico. As cross-border workers, they earn American dollars and can directly purchase groceries and other household goods with their earnings and take these purchases with them to Mexico. Their employment allows them the financial resources to become consumers on the American side of the border, which is a privilege for only a few in the Mexican working class. Unlike long-term migrants, who send money home to support their families and often have little input or control on how this money is spent, border crossers are able to control how their earnings are spent. With their earnings, they themselves made decisions on how to spend this money by directly purchasing household goods at the Laredo downtown before returning to their homes in Nuevo Laredo.

Everyday, thousands of people enter the Laredo port to shop, visit, or work. The city of Laredo benefits from the revenue these visitors bring to the city. Cross-border workers enter the U.S. under the guise of shopping. My conversations with cross-border domestic workers revealed that border officials are aware that women enter the U.S. with border-crossing visas for the purpose of undocumented labor in the U.S. I found that border officials facilitate this movement by either turning a blind eye or by knowingly hiring these women to work in their own homes. Employers also facilitate their crossing by creating a demand for this labor and in some cases, taking an active interest in ensuring their employee's safe movement across the border.

Once cross-border domestic workers enter Laredo, their legality and consequent freedoms as border inhabitants fluctuates depending on the different spaces of the border cities that they inhabit. I rely on the notion of "transnational social spaces" to understand the different social meanings of space across national boundaries. I found that in the journey cross-border workers take to and from work, they enter and exit multiple "safe" and "risky" spaces. When they cross the bridge into Laredo and enter the downtown, they are in a part of the city that is dominated by Mexican shoppers. Downtown Laredo is a safe space where they blend in with other pedestrians and shoppers; but as they leave the downtown to travel to their workplaces in neighborhoods across the city, their identities shift from consumers to producers/workers. Once these women gather at bus stops and enter residential neighborhoods, their nationality, class, and gender expose them as undocumented workers in this city.

Crossing the multiple borders of safe and risky spaces in Laredo violates the conditions of their entry, which puts them at a greater risk of discovery and/or apprehension.

Once they have reached employers' homes, cross-border workers feel safe since they are away from public view, yet this is precisely where they violate the terms of their visas by working for pay. Employers' and border officials' make similar moves through the social space of the city; since once they employ cross-border workers they shift from being productive workers to consumers in the local economy. Thus, I found that time and space has social meanings that affect cross-border workers as well as border officials and employers.

The social actors interacting with these cross-border domestic workers are revealed in the narratives of cross-border domestic workers— border guards who allow them to enter, often knowing they are planning to violate the terms of their visa, and employers, who are also often border officials, who create a demand for this migrant labor. The examination of the multiple spaces they inhabit reveal that although these women empowered themselves by finding a means to become cross-border workers and successfully enter the United States, the very act of working without official documents has subverted their intention to travel across Laredo without suspicion, so much so that even when domestic workers enter Laredo without the intention of working, they continue to feel vulnerable across different spaces in Laredo. The consumption of their labor by border officials also complicates meaning and location of safe and risky spaces in the city. Domestic workers are aware that border officials are violating the terms of their employment when they employ undocumented labor and therefore are also at risk of discovery. In these relationships, cross-border workers are in a position of power in which they too can "out" their employer.

In addition to successfully navigating these transnational border spaces, cross-border domestic workers must develop social networks that also cross the international divide. Locating and securing employment in this occupation involves finding and maintaining contacts with women on both sides of the border. Often these employment opportunities traveled through family networks, specifically from mother to daughter. Employers also had to develop networks that crossed borders in order to find "good," reliable workers. Cross-border workers who have an established network are at the center of this economy of domestic work. I found that locating a job entails the movement of knowledge across these transnational spaces, which span across geographic and political divides.

The demand for domestic labor in Laredo is a driving force in women's determination to cross borders to labor in this occupation. For border residents, the practice of having hired household help in the home is part of this border zone/culture. In this city, the jobs associated with being a "maid" involve housekeeping, housecleaning, nanny work, ironing, and elderly care. In Laredo, middle and upper-class employers seek out the inexpensive labor of Mexican women to care for their aging parents; these workers provide the personal attention often not available in nursing homes without the expense of full-time nursing care. Cross-border workers and immigrant workers at the border fill this demand and care for children and the elderly, often at the sacrifice of caring for their own families.

In addition to examining the different occupations involved in domestic labor at the border, I also explored the relationships between cross-border domestic workers and employers. In past studies on domestic work, scholars have examined the intersections of race, class, and gender in the relationships between these two groups of women to understand the power dynamics between them, and how the intersection of these social categories affects their respective privileges and disadvantages (Rollins 1988; Romero 1992; Dill 1988; Hondagneu-Sotelo 2001). Since these studies have primarily focused on white employers and Black or Latina domestic workers, race and class have been used to conceptualize the hierarchies and inequalities embedded in these relationships. This study takes a different approach: since employers and employees are co-ethnic, I have used national belonging rather than race as a key analytic through which I examine employee/employer dynamics. I rely on Michele Lamont's (1992) theory of symbolic boundaries to understand the hierarchies of gender, class, and nationality that are created by employers at the workplace. I found that employers produce these boundaries through the management and control of food in their homes. Boundaries were created through the denial and restriction of food, the provision of lower quality food for workers, and the segregation of workers during mealtimes; they worked to communicate class inequalities between employers and domestic workers in the workplace. Since Mexican domestic workers and Mexican American employers share a common ethnicity, it is possible to single out differences of social class apart from considerations of race that have been the focus of past studies. The poverty that is associated with Mexico and which lies just across the border is inflected through class differences that are communicated by employers to their workers. The separation of food and persons at mealtimes that employers enforce represents deep class divides that are apparent across this Third World/First World divide at the border. Mexican cross-border workers are understood as a part of Mexico, which is viewed as culturally rich but also as poor, corrupt, and violent, creating a national divide at the workplace. In other words, nationality serves a form of racialization that separates workers from employers by class. I found that class relations between women employers and domestic workers are (re)produced through gendered notions of ethnicity and nationality that are mobilized by both workers and employers. For example, while the narratives of domestic workers living in Nuevo Laredo focused on their styles of mothering and cooking to claim identities as authentic 'Mexican' women, employers in the United States constructed narratives to distinguish themselves from their domestics who, they often viewed as having indigenous style of dressing.

Since domestic workers lacked control over the material practices of food, they created symbolic boundaries that expressed their superiority over employers who had economic advantages. These boundaries were produced through the constructs of ideal womanhood and the "authentic" Mexican woman. In so doing, they communicate the ideals that they value as Mexican women relative to their Mexican American employers, who they see as being overly influenced by the American way of life. They critiqued their employers for adopting American values and practices, such as over indulging their children and valuing consumption over motherhood. Ironically, workers did not recognize that they were also practicing aspects of the "American" way of life that they were critical of, since they were also away from their children for most of the day, and they valued the privilege of shopping in Laredo. Hence, Mexican domestic workers constructed gendered meanings of nationality to legitimize to enable them to cope with the degradation of selfhood produced through the intimate practices of domestic labor. By analyzing these two groups of co-ethnic women, this study examined the multiple and intersecting meanings of gender, class, and nationality in the employer/employee relationship. This intersectional perspective on the experiences of Mexican workers and Mexican American employers reflects gendered constructions of nationality and ethnicity that work to produce, and reproduce, class differences between maids and their employers.

The findings in this study are relevant to the sociological literature on migration and the interdisciplinary literature on women's migration. Although this study focuses on cross-border laborers who reside in Mexico and enter the United States temporarily, these findings are relevant for studies of other forms of temporary migration, such as "non-immigrant" H1-B workers in the United States. In addition, recent literature on migration has re-conceptualized the notion of "legal" and "illegal" (Menjivar 2006); this study adds to that line of scholarship in my analysis of space and the fluctuating legality cross-border workers experience as they traverse to and from work in the border city of Laredo. Additionally, my findings on the shifting identities of workers from consumers to producers, and the subsequent shift of employers and border officers from productive workers to positions as consumers extends the notion of transnational space from its current conception across large geographic areas and national boundaries to multiple spaces within border zones, which are in close geographic proximity but across national divides.

This study is also relevant to the literature on domestic service. With the global migration of women across the world, this literature has changed its focus from documenting the labor of domestic service and the experiences of North American women (Palmer 1989; Katzman 1981; Rollins 1985; Romero 1992) to including the migrant experiences of women in this occupation (Hondagneu-Sotelo 2001; Parreñas 2001). This study documents the migratory labor experiences of Mexican cross-border domestic workers and provides a context for understanding their opportunities and lifestyles in Mexico. Finally, the findings of this study also are relevant to the interdisciplinary literature on borders and borderlands. In this study, I seek to understand borders as both political and geographic as well metaphorical. On a daily basis, the domestic workers in this study confront and cross the national border that divides these two countries as well as the symbolic boundaries in employers' homes.

Limitations of this Study and Future Research

As a qualitative study on the labor migration of Mexican domestic workers, this study did not aim to produce generalizable findings on Mexican women migrants or on migratory patterns in cities across the U.S.-Mexico border. This study follows past literature on domestic service, which typically relies on qualitative methods to capture the experiences of this unexposed population. Due to the limitations of time and the scope of this study, I only interviewed women. In future research, I am interested in including men who also cross borders for labor in my sample. This inclusion can provide a more informative analysis of the role of gender in this migration process. For future research, I might also consider a multi-sample study with long-term immigrants and cross-border domestic workers. My original research design included this comparison, but when I was in the field, I discovered that this population is difficult to reach. As a result, the immigrant women's sub-sample was too small to make a comparative case with the cross-border sample. Nonetheless, I consider my findings valid for Mexican women cross-domestics in Laredo, with potential relevance to all border cities.

Finally, in future research I would also like to analyze the notion of citizenship along with nationality. The pro-immigrant marches in major cities across the United States in 2006 have justified immigrants belonging to the United States through the idea of "social citizenship" and have drawn researchers to conceptualize citizenship beyond political communities (Del Castillo 2008). Cross-border workers are not citizens of the United States but their pseudo-legal status complicates their belonging in that they can claim certain rights as consumers and border visitors. In addition, since domestic workers and employers share both ethnicity and language, legal citizenship shapes who becomes a domestic worker.

The Future of Cross-Border Domestic Work

Since the time I left the field at the end of 2005, anti-immigrant sentiment has reached an all-time high and has received a significant amount of media attention. As a reaction to these attitudes, in 2006 immigrants, immigrant sympathizers, and their families marched across major cities to show their presence and protest their criminalization. But the implications for undocumented entry have dramatically changed in the last few years— immigrant raids at places of employment have increased and been widely publicized, cities are enacting anti-immigrant legislation, and detention centers are being filled with persons caught living in this country without legal documentation. In 2006, the Comprehensive Immigration and Reform Act, which proposed to allow undocumented immigrants living in the United States to become naturalized, and which also called for a guest worker program for non-agricultural Mexican workers, failed to become law. Academics have called for similar policy changes that would legalize Mexican workers and provide the legal entry of low-skilled workers in addition to the high-skilled workers that are favored in current immigration policies (Cornelius 2006). However, legislators fear that, like the Bracero Program, a guest-worker program would trigger more undocumented immigration.

This anti-immigrant sentiment and the struggle to control the 2,000 mile border is impacting the crossing patterns of local Mexican residents— both those who enter border cities to visit and those who enter to work. Entry from Mexico is increasingly becoming more difficult with lines at the border getting longer and opportunities for legal entry becoming more limited. Plans to track cross-border entries and exits have not yet been implemented, but are slated to become part of the larger picture of "border security." Currently, the entry of cross-border workers, although widely known by border officials, is not a major area of reform and is considered a part of border life; but as these borders continue to tighten, the entry of daily visitors from Mexico could also be limited or completely blocked. These changes will cripple border economies, such as Laredo, that economically depend on the revenues these shoppers bring to the city as well as the cheap labor these communities have come to depend upon. In my conversations with cross-border workers, I asked them what they would do if they could no longer cross into Laredo. Some women were optimistic about their abilities to support their families. Esperanza Salazar, who worked as live-in caretaker for an elderly couple, said:

> I would work here [Nuevo Laredo]. I have many ways to make money. I could sell tamales or sell lunches. My original plans was not to work [in Laredo] on the weekends and instead make tamales to sell. So I was planning to make tamales anyways. Just the other day I was going to make menudo to sell to my neighbors, so I will find a way to survive.

Most cross-border workers did not share this optimism. Lilia Garcia, who also cares for an elderly couple in Laredo and supports her husband and daughter, became anxious when I asked about the future of cross-border work:

> I don't know what I would do if I couldn't cross. I try not to think of those things because my crossing card is my salary and it is also what my daughter lives on, because she is still in school. I guess I would look for work here [Nuevo Laredo]. I don't know what would happen. I don't want to think about it right now.

Rosie Sanchez, who works as a housecleaner four days a week in Laredo, was taken by surprise when I asked this question:

> My life would change completely! The thing is that I'm so used to going over there to earn money, because here they pay so much less. Finding other work, like factory work here [in Nuevo Laredo], wouldn't even make sense for me with what I pay my mother in-law for daycare. I'm not working to support my mother in-law! With what I would earn in the factory and with what I pay my mother in-law, I would only be left with 100 pesos a day [approximately $10]. What do I do with 100 pesos? That is why my life would dramatically change.

Lupe Martinez, who works as a caretaker for the elderly on the weekends, expressed her feelings best when she said:

> I would be very upset [me daria mucho coraje] if I couldn't cross because we don't deserve this. When my husband was working, I didn't need the job so much because with his bonus [at the factory] we would buy clothes and other things we needed. I would be very upset if I couldn't shop anymore too. I don't want that to ever happen and I don't think God wants that to happen either.

Cross-border domestic workers are not the only group that depends on entering the United States to maintain their livelihoods. Gardeners, flea-market vendors, street vendors, and others depend on their entry into the United States to work or buy goods for their small businesses in Nuevo Laredo. Pressures to limit the working class Mexican from temporarily visiting the United States will alter the way of life in these communities and of these workers who depend on this international movement to sustain their families.

Bibliography

Aguilar, J. 1981. "Insider Research: An Ethnography of a
    Debate." Pp. 15-28 in Anthropologists at Home in
    North America: Methods and Issues in the Study of
    One's Own Society, edited by D. Messerschmidt.
    Cambridge: Cambridge University Press.
Alegria, T. 2002. "Demand and Supply of Mexican Cross-
    Border Workers." Journal of Borderland Studies 17:37-
    55.
Amir, T. 1993. "BP Chief: No Time to Go After Mexican
    Maids." The Laredo Morning Times, Sept. 09. Laredo,
    Texas.
Andreas, P. 2000. Border Games: Policing the U.S.-Mexico
    Divide. Cornell: Cornell University Press.
—. 2003. "A Tale of Two Borders: The U.S. - Canada and
    U.S.-Mexico Lines after 9-11." Pp. 1-23 in The
    Rebordering of North America, edited by P. Andreas
    and T. J. Biersteker. New York: Routledge.
Anzaldua, G. 1987. Borderlands/La Frontera: the New
    Mestiza. San Francisco: Spinsters/Aunt Lute.
Aysa, M., & D. S. Massey. 2004. "Wives Left Behind: The
    Labor Market Behavior of Women in Migrant
    Communities." In Crossing the Border: Research from
    the Mexican Migration Project, edited by J. Durand &
    D. S. Massey New York: Russell Sage Foundation.

171

Basch, L., N.G. Schiller, & C. S. Blanc. 1994. Nations Unbound: Transnational Projects, Postcolonial Predicaments, and Deterritorialized Nation-States. Langhorne: Gordon and Breach.

Batalova, J. 2008. "US in Focus: Mexican Immigration in the United States." Migration Information Source: Fresh Thought, Authoritative Data, Global Reach (http://www.migrationinformation.org/USfocus).

Bean, F.D., G. Vernez, & C.B. Keely. 1989. Opening and Closing the Doors: Evaluating Immigration Reform and Control. Washington D.C.: Urban Institute.

Behar, R. 1993. Translated Woman: Crossing the Border with Esparanza's Story. Boston: Beacon Press.

Bever, S.W. 2002. 'Migration and the Transformation of Gender Roles and Hierarchies in Yucatan.' Urban Anthropology and Studies of Cultural Systems and World Economic Development 31 (2):199-131.

Bouwens, S. 2004. "The Dynamics of Cross-Border Labor: Commuting from the Dutch to the German Part of the Euregio Meuse-Rhine, 1960-2000." Journal of Borderlands Studies 19:135-153.

Brezosky, L. 2007. "Merchants Say Whole Class of Shoppers Has Disappeared." Laredo Morning Times, 2006.

Brownell, P.B. 2010. "Wage Differences between Temporary and Permanent Immigrants." International Migration Review 44: 593-694.

Bulbeck, C. 1998. Re-orienting Western Feminisms: Women's Diversity in a Postcolonial World. Cambridge: New York: Cambridge University Press.

Burawoy, M. 1991. "Introduction." In Ethnography Unbound: Power and Resistance in the Modern

Metropolis, edited by M. Burawoy et al. Pp. 1-7. Berkeley: University of California Press.

Cerrutti, M., & D. S. Massey. 2001. "On the Auspices of Female Migration from Mexico to the United States." Demography 38:187-200.

——. 2004. Trends in Mexican Migration to the United States, 1965 to 1995. In Crossing the Border: Research from the Mexican Migration Project, edited by J. Durand & D. S. Massey. New York: Russell Sage Foundation.

Chang, G. 2000. Disposable Domestics: Immigrant Women Workers in the Global Economy. Cambridge: South End Press.

Collins, Patricia. 1986. "Learning from the Outsider Within: The Sociological Significance of Black Feminist Thought." Social Problems 33:14-32.

——. 1990. Black Feminist Though: Knowledge, Consciousness, and the Politics of Empowerment. London: HarperCollins Academic.

——. 1994. Shifting the Center: Race, Class, and FeministTheorizing about Motherhood. New York: Routledge.

Constable, N. 1997. Maid to Order in Hong Kong: Stories of Filipina Workers. Ithaca: Cornell University Press.

Cornelius, W. A. 1992. "From Sojourners to Settlers: The Changing Profile of Mexican Immigration to the United States." In U.S.-Mexico Relations: Labor Market Interdependence, edited by J. A. Bustamante, C. W. Reynolds & R. Hinojosa Ojeda. Stanford: Stanford University Press.

Cornelius, W. A. 2001. "Death at the Border: Efficacy and Unintended Consequences of U.S. Immigration to the

United States." Population and Development Review 27:661-85.

—. 2007. "Introduction: Does Border Enforcement Deter Unauthorized Immigration." in Impacts of Border Enforcement on Mexican Migration, edited by W. A. Cornelius and J. M. Lewis. La Jolla: Center for Comparative Immigration Studies, UCSD.

Cowan, R. S. 1983. More Work for Mother: the Ironies of Household Technology from the Open Hearth to the Microwave. New York: Basic Books.

Craig, R. B. 1971. The Bracero Program: Interest Groups and Foreign Policy. Austin: University of Texas Press.

Crenshaw, K. W. 1995. "The Intersection of Race and Gender." In Critical Race Theory, edited by Crenshaw et al. Pp. 357-383. New York: The New York Press.

de Certeau, M. 1984. The Practice of Everyday Life. Berkeley: University of California Press.

de la Luz Ibarra, M. 2000. "Mexican Immigrant Women and the New Domestic Labor." Human Organization 59:452-64.

Del Castillo, A. R. 2007. "Illegal Status and Social Citizenship: Thoughts on Mexican Immigrants in a Postnational World." Pp. 92-105 in Women and Migration in the U.S.-Mexico Borderlands, edited by D. A. Segura & P. Zavella. Durham & London: Duke University Press.

Denzin, N. & Y. Lincoln. 1994. Handbook of Qualitative Research. Thousand Oaks: Sage.

Dill, B. T. 1988. "Making Your Job Good Yourself": Domestic Service and the Construction of Personal Dignity. Philadelphia: Temple University Press.

Diner, H. 1983. Erin's Daughter in America. Baltimore: Johns Hopkins University Press.

Donato, K., E. Patterson, J. Duran, & D. S. Massey. 2004. "Women and Men on the Move: Undocumented Border Crossing." Pp. 111-130 in Crossing the Border: Research from the Mexican Migration Project, edited by J. Durand & D.S. Massey. New York: Russell Sage Foundation.

Donato, K. M. 1993. Current Trends and Patterns of Female Migration: Evidence from Mexico. International Migration Review 27 (4):748-771.

Durand, J., W. Kandel, E. A. Parrado, & D. S. Massey 1996. "International Migration and Development in Mexican Communities." Demography 33:249-64.

Durand, J., D. S. Massey, & R. M. Zenteno. 2001. "Mexican Immigration to the United States: Continuities and Change." Latín American Research Review 36 (1):107-127.

Durand, J., D. S. Massey, & E. A. Parrado. 1999. The New Era of Mexican Migration to the United States. The Journal of American History 86 (2): 518-36.

Ehrenreich, B., and A. R. Hochschild. 2000. "Introduction." Pp. 1-14 in Global Woman: Nannies, Maids, and Sex Workers in the New Economy, edited by B. Ehrenreich and A. R. Hochschild. New York: Harry Hold and Company, LLC.

Emerson, R., R. Fretz, & L. Shaw.1995. Writing Ethnographic Fieldnotes. Chicago: University of Chicago Press.

Eschbach, K., J. Hagan, N. Rodriguez, R. Hernandez-Leon, & S. Bailey. 1999. "Death at the Border." The International Migration Review 33:430-455.

Faist, T. 2000. The Volume and Dynamics of International
    Migration and Transnational Social Spaces. Oxford:
    Clarendon Press.
Fernandez-Kelly, M. P. 1983. For We Are Sold: I and My
    People. Albany: State University New York Press.
Fry, R. 2006. "Gender and Migration." Report. Pew
    Hispanic Center, Washington D.C.
Gibbs, N. 2000. "A Whole New World: Along the U.S.-
    Mexico Border where Hearts and Minds and Money
    and Culture Merge, the Century of the Americas is
    Born." Pp. 36-47 in Times.
Glenn, E N. (Ed.). 1994. Social Construction of Mothering:
    A Thematic Overview. New York: Routledge.
Glenn, E. N. 1986. Issei, Nisei, War Bride :
    ThreeGenerations of Japanese American Women in
    Domestic Service. Philadelphia: Temple University
    Press.
—. 1992. "From Servitude to Service Work:
    HistoricalContinuities in the Racial Division of Paid
    Reproductive Labor." Signs 18:1-43.
—. 2002. Unequal Freedom: How Race and GenderShaped
    American Citizenship and Labor. Cambridge: Harvard
    University Press.
Glick Schiller, N., L. Basch, & C. Blanc-Szanton.
    1992.Towards a Transnational Perspective on
    Migration: Race, Class, Ethnicity, and Nationalism
    Reconsidered. New York: New York Academy of
    Social Science.
Gonzalez de la Rocha, M. 1993. "El Poder de la
    Ausencia:Mujeres y Migracion en una Communidad de
    los Altos de Jalisco." In Las Realidades Regionales de
    la Crisis Nacional. Zamora: Michoacan.

Grasmuck, S, and P. Pessar. 1991. Between Two Islands:Dominican International Migration. Berkeley: University of California Press.

Guendelman, S., and A. Perez-Itriaga. 1987. 'Double Lives: The Changing Role of Women in Seasonal Migration." Women Studies 13: 249-71.

Hall, M. 2006. "Cross-border Shoppers Important to Economy." in Laredo Morning Times. Laredo. http://madmax.lmtonline.com/textarchives/12306/j20.

Hansen, R. D. 1971. The Politics of Mexican Development. Baltimore: Johns Hopkins University Press.

Herzog, L. A. 1990. "Border Commuter Workers and Transfrontier Metropolitan Structure along the United States-Mexico Border." Journal of Borderland Studies 5:1-20.

Hirsch, J. S. 1999. "En el Norte la Mujer Manda: Gender, Generation, and Geography in a Mexican Transnational Community." The American Behavioral Scientist 42:1332-1350.

—. "Que Pues, con el Pinche NAFTA?" Urban Anthropology and Studies of Cultural Systems and World Economic Development 31 (3-4):351-388.

Hondagneu-Sotelo, P. 1994a. Gendered Transitions: Mexican Experiences of Immigration. Berkeley: University of California Press.

—. 2001. Domestica: Immigrant Workers Cleaning and Caring in the Shadows of Affluence. Berkeley: University of California Press.

—. 2003. "Gender and Immigration: A Retrospective and Introduction." Pp. 3-19 in Gender and U.S. Migration: Contemporary Trends, edited by P. Hondagneu-Sotelo.

Berkeley & Los Angeles: University of California Press.

Hondagneu-Sotelo, P., & E. Avila. 1997. " 'I'm Here, But I'm There': The Meanings of Transnational Motherhood." Gender & Society 11:548-571.

Katzman, D. 1981. Seven Days a Week: Women and Domestic Service in Industrializing America. Urbana: University Of Illinois Press.

Kibria, Nazli. 1993. The Family Tightrope: The Changing Lives of Vietnamese Americans. Princeton: Princeton University Press.

Kiser, G. C., and M. W. Kiser. 1979. "Mexican Commuters." in Mexican Workers in the United States: Historical and Political Perspectives, edited by G. C. Kiser & M. W. Kiser. Albuquerque: University of New Mexico Press.

Kopinak, K. 1995. "Gender as a Vehicle for the Subordination of Women Maquiladora Workers in Mexico." Latin American Perspectives 22:30-48.

Koussoudji, S. A., and S. I. Ranney. 1984. "The Labor Market Experience of Female Migrants: The Case of Temporary Mexican Migration to the U.S." International Migration Review 18 (4):1120-1143.

Lal, J. 1998. "Situating Location(s): The Politics of Self, Identity, and the "Other" in Living and Writing the Text." Pp. 100-137 in Feminist Approaches to Theory and Methodology: An Interdisciplinary Reader, edited by S. Hesse-Biber, C. Gilmartin, & R. Lydenberg. New York: Oxford University Press.

Lamont, M. 1992. Money, Morals, and Manners: The Culture of the French and American Upper-Middle Class. University of Chicago: Chicago.

Lan, P. 2006. Global Cinderellas: Migrant Domestics and Newly Rich Employers in Taiwan. Durham: Duke University Press.

Lefebvre, H. 1991. The Production of Space. Cambridge: Basil Blackwell.

Levitt P., and N. G. Schiller. 2004. "Conceptualizing Simultaneity: A Transnational Social Field Perspective on Society." International Migration Review 38:1002-39.

Levitt, P. 2003. "Transnational Migration and the Redefinition of the State: Variations and Explanations." Ethnic and Racial Studies 26:587-611.

Levitt P., & N. Jaworsky. 2007. "Transnational Migration Studies: Past Developments and Future Trends." Annual Review of Sociology 33:129-156.

Lichter, D.T. & Johnson, K.M. 2009. "Immigrant Gateways and Hispanic Migration to New Destinations" 43:496-518.

Lindstrom, D. P. 1996. "Economic Opportunity in Mexico and Return Migration from the United States." Demography 33 (3):357-374. Loaeza, S. 2006. "Problems of Political Consolidation in Mexico." In Changing Structure of Mexico, edited by L. Randall. Armonk: M.E. Sharpe.

Lofland, J. & L. H. Lofland. 1995. Analyzing Social Settings: A Guide to Qualitative Observation and Analysis. San Francisco: Wadsworth Publishing Company.

Mahler, Sarah J. 2003. "Engendering Transnational Migration: A Case Study of Salvadorians." Pp. 187-317 in Gender and U.S. Immigration: Contemporary

Trends, edited by P. Hondagneu-Sotelo Berkeley & Los Angeles: University of California Press.

Mahler, S. J., and P. R. Pessar. 2001. "Gendered Geographies of Power: Analyzing Gender across Transnational Spaces." Identities: Global Studies in Culture and Power 7:441-459.

Martin, P. 2007. Migration News 14: 4. http://migration.ucdavis.edu/mn/more.php?id=3321_0_2_0.

Massey D. 1994. Space, Place, and Gender. Minneapolis: University of Minnesota Press.

Massey, D. S. 1999. International Migration at the Dawn of the Twenty-First Century: the Role of the State. Population and Development Review 25:303-23.

Massey D. S., J. Durand, & N. J. Malone. 2002. Beyond Smoke and Mirrors: Mexican Immigration in an Era of Economic Integration. New York: Russell Sage Foundation.

Massey, D. S., & K. E. Espinosa. 1997. What's Driving Mexico-U.S. Migration? A Theoretical, Empirical, and Policy Analysis. The American Journal of Sociology 102 (4):939-999.

Mattingly, D. J. 1999. "Job Search, Social Networks, and Local Labor-Market Dynamics: the Case of Paid Household Work in San Diego, California." Urban Geography 20:46-74.

Menjivar, C. 2006. "Liminal Legality: Salvadoran and Guatemalan Immigrants' Lives in the United States." American Journal of Sociology 111:999-1037.

Mines, R., & D. S. Massey. 1985. Patterns and Migration to the United States from Two Mexican Communities. Latin American Research Review 20:104-124.

Mintz, S. W., & C. M. Du Bois. 2002. "The Anthropology of Food and Eating." Annual Review of Anthropology 31:99-119.

Momsem, J. H. 1999. "Maids on the Move." Pp. 1-20 in Gender, Migration, and Domestic Service, edited by J. H. Momsem. London: Routledge.

Mooney, M. 2003. "Migrants' Social Ties in the U.S. and Investment in Mexico." Social Forces 81:1147-70.

Nagar, Richa. 1997. "Exploring the Methodological Borders through Oral Narratives." Pp. 203-224 in Thresholds in Feminist Geography, edited by J. P. Jones III, H. J. Nast & S. M. Roberts. Lanham: Rowman and Littlefield Publishers Inc.

Narayan, K. 1993. "How Native Is a "Native" Anthropologist?" American Anthropologist 95:671-86.

Ong, A. 1999. Flexible Citizenship: The Cultural Logics of Transnationality. Durham and London: Duke University Press.

Orrenius, P. M. 1994. "The Effect of U.S. Border Enforcement on the Crossing Behavior of Mexican Migrants." in Crossing the Border: Research from the Mexican Migration Project, edited by J. Durand & D. S. Massey. New York: Russell Sage Foundation.

Owen, C. 2002. "Mixed Outlook: Study Examines Laredo after a Decade of Growth." in The Laredo Morning Times. Laredo.

Palmer, P. M. 1989. Domesticity and Dirt: Housewives and Domestic Servants in the United States, 1920-1945 Philadelphia Temple University Press.

Parrado, E. A., & C. Flippen. 2005. "Migration and Gender among Mexican Women." American Sociological Review 70 (4): 606-632.

Parreñas, R. S. 2001. Servants of Globalization: Women, Migration and Domestic Work. Stanford: Stanford University Press.

—. 2008. The Force of Domesticity: Filipina Migrants and Globalization. New York: NYU Press.

Passel, J. 2006. "Size and Characteristics of the Unauthorized Migrant Populations in the United States: Estimates Based on the March 2005 Current Population Survey." Washington D.C.: Pew Hispanic Research Center.

Pedraza S. 1991. "Women and Migration: The Social Consequences of Gender." Annual Review of Sociology 17:303-325.

Pessar P. R. 1999. "Engendering Migration Studies: The Case of New Immigrants in the United States." The American Behavioral Scientist 42:577-601.

Pessar P. R., & S. J. Mahler. 2003. "Transnational Migration: Bringing Gender In." The International Migration Review 37:812-35.

Pisani, Michael J., and David W. Yoskowitz. 2001. "'Por Necesidad' -Transnational Labor Movements, Informality and Wage Determination: An Exploratory Study of Maids on the U.S.-Mexican Border." Journal of Borderlands Studies 16 (1):67-82.

—. 2002. "The Maid Trade: Cross-Border Work in South Texas." Social Science Quarterly 83 (2):568-579.

—. 2005. "Grass, Sweat, and Sun: An Exploratory Study of the Labor Market for Gardeners in South Texas." Social Science Quarterly 86:230-251.

Portes, A., L. E. Guarnizo, & P. Landolt. 1999. "The Study of Transnationalism: Pitfalls and Promise of an Emergent Research Field." Ethnic and Racial Studies 22:217-23.

Prieto, N. I. 1997. Beautiful Flowers of the Maquiladora: Life Histories of Women Workers in Tijuana. Austin: University of Texas Press.

Qayum, S., & R. Ray. 2003. "Grappling with Modernity: India's Respectable Classes and the Culture of Domestic Servitude." Ethnography 4(4): 520-555.

Quintanilla, M. & Peter Copeland. 1996. "Mexican Maids: El Paso's Worst Kept Secret." In U.S. Borderlands: Historical and Contemporary Perspectives, edited by O. J. Martinez. Delaware: Scholarly Resources.

Ramirez, M. T. 2001a. "Crossers Facing Long Lines, Checks." in The Laredo Morning Times. Sept. 18. Laredo, Texas.

—. 2001b. "Crossing Cards Confiscated at Laredo Bridge." The Laredo Morning Times. Sept. 19. Laredo, Texas.

Reinharz, S. 1992. Feminist Methods in Social Science Research. New York: Oxford University Press.

Reyes, B., H. P. Johnson, & R.V. Swearigen. 2002. Holding the Line? - The Effect of the Recent Border Build-up on Unauthorized Immigration. San Francisco: Public Policy Institute of California.

Richards, A. 2008. "Border Residents, Officials Fear Longer Bridge Lines." in The Laredo Morning Times. Laredo.

Richardson, C. 1999. Batos, Bolillos, Pochos, & Pelados: Class and Culture on the South Texas Border. Austin: Univeristy of Texas Press.

Robinson, Jennifer. 1994. "White Women Researching/Representing "Others": From Antiapartheid to Postcolonialism?" Pp. 197-229 in Writing, Women, and Space, edited by A. B. & G. Rose. New York and London: The Guliford Press.

Rollins, J. 1985. Between Women: Domestics and their Employers. Philadelphia: Temple University Press.

Romero, M. 1992. Maid in the U.S.A. New York: Routledge.

Romero, M. 1988. "Chicanas Modernize Domestic Service." Qualitative Sociology 11:319-334.

Rosaldo, R. 1989. Culture and Truth: The Remaking of Social Analysis. Boston: Beacon Press.

Rouse, R. 1995. "Questions of Identity: Personhood and Collectivity in Transnational Migration to the United States." Critique of Anthropology 15:351-380.

Rouse, R. 1992. "Making Sense of Settlement: Class Transformation, Cultural Struggle, and Transnationalism among Mexican Migrants in the United States." Annals of the New York Academy of Sciences, 645: 25-52.

Ruiz, V. L. 1987. "By the Day or the Week: Mexicana Domestic Workers in El Paso." Pp. 61-76 in Women on the U.S.-Mexico Border, edited by Vicky L. Ruiz and Susan Tiano. Boston: Allen & Unwin.

Salzinger, L. 2003. Genders in Production: Making Workers in Mexico's Global Factories. Berkeley and Los Angeles University of California Press.

Sassen, S. 2003. "Global Cities and Survival Circuits." in Global Woman, edited by Ehrenreich, B. & A. R. Hoschschild. New York: Metropolitan Books.

Sassen S. 1998a. "America's Immigration "Problem"." in Globalization and Its Discontents: Essays on the New Mobility of People and Money by S. Sassen. New York: The New York Press.

—. 1998b. "Notes on the Incorporation of Third World Women into Wage Labor through Immigration and Offshore Production." in Globalization and Its

Discontents: Essays on the New Mobility of People and Money. New York: New York Press.

Schack, M. 2000. "Cross-Border Commuting and Integration." in Northern European Baltic Integration: Yearbook 2000, edited by L. Hedelund & B. Lindstroem. Berlin and New York: Springer.

Segura, D. A. 1994. "Inside the Work Worlds of Chicana and Mexican Immigrant Women." in Women of Color in U.S. Society, edited by B. M. Zinn & Bonnie Thornton Dill. Philadelphia: Temple University Press.

Sheahan, J. 1991. Conflict and Change in Mexican Economic Strategy Implications for Mexico and Latin America. La Jolla: University of California San Diego, Center for U.S.-Mexican Studies.

Singer, A., & D. S. Massey. 1998. "The Social Process of Undocumented Border Crossing Among Mexican Migrants." International Migration Review 32:561-592.

Smith, M. P. 2005. "Transnationalism Unbound." Journal of Ethnic and Migration Studies 31:235-244.

Spradley, J. 1979. The Ethnographic Interview. New York: Holt. Rinehart & Winston.

Steinberg, S. 1981. "Why Irish Became Domestics and Italians and Jews Did Not." Pp. 151-168 in The Ethnic Myth: Race, Ethnicity, and Class in America, edited by Anonymous. Boston: Beacon Press.

Spener, D., & K. Staudt. 1998. "The View from the Frontier: Theoretical Perspectives Undisciplined." in The U.S.-Mexico Border: Transcending Division, Contesting Identities, edited by D. Spener & K. Staudt. Boulder: Lynne Rienner Publishers.

Staudt, Kathleen. 1998. Free Trade? Informal Economies at the U.S.-Mexico Border. Philadelphia: Temple University Press.

Sutherland, D. E. 1981. Americans and their Servants: Domestic Service in the United States from 1800 to 1920. Baton Rouge: London: Louisiana State University Press.

Thompson, G. 2005a. ""Drug Violence Paralyzes a City, and Chills the Border." in The New York Times. New York. into a War Zone." in The New York Times. New York.

Tiano, S. 1994. Patriarchy on the line: Labor, Gender, and Ideology in the Mexican Maquila Industry. Philadelphia: Temple University Press.

United Nations. 1990. "United Nations Convention on the Protection of the Rights of All Migrant Workers and Members of their Families." http://www.un.org/documents/ga/res/45/a45r158.htm

U.S. Bureau of Economic Analysis. 2006. "Regional Economic Accounts." http://www.bea.gov/regional/bearfacts/action.cfm?yeari n=2006&areatype=MSA&fips=29700.

United States Department of State. 2002. "Border Crossing Card (BCC) Page." http://www.travel.state.gov/visa/temp/types/types_1266 .html

United States Department of Transportation. 2007. "Bureau of Transportation Statistics." http://www.transtats.bts.gov/bordercrossings.

Vila, P. 2003. "The Limits of American Border Theory." in Ethnography at the Border, edited by P. Vila. Minneapolis: University of Minnesota Press.

Vo, L. 2000. "Performing Ethnography in Asian American Communities: Beyond the Insider-Verses-Outsider Perspective." Pp. 17-37 in Cultural Compass: Ethnographic Explorations of Asian America, edited by

M. Manalansan IV. Philadelphia: Temple University Press.

Weiss, R.S. 1995. Learning from Strangers: The Art and Method of Qualitative Interview Studies. New York: Free Press.

Wrigley, Julia. 1995. Other People's Children. New York: Basic Books. U.S. Census Bureau. 2006.http://www.census.gov/ popest/cities/ SUB-EST2006.html

Zavella, P. 1993. "Feminist Insider Dilemmas: Constructing Ethnic Identity with "Chicana" Informants." Frontiers XIII: 53-75.

Index

CPSIA information can be obtained at www.ICGtesting.com
Printed in the USA
BVOW042115230512

290763BV00003B/1/P